The Super-Green Clean

The Super-Green Clean

Using Microfiber Towels to Clean Almost Anything with Plain Water

By Appaloosa Moose

Rafter-four Designs
Cocolalla, Idaho

**The Super-Green Clean
Using Microfiber Towels
to Clean Almost Anything
with Plain Water**

Rafter-four Designs

For information address:
Rafter-four Designs
P O Box 40
Cocolalla, ID 83813

ISBN: 1-931426-40-6

Printed in the United States of America

THE SUPER-GREEN CLEAN:
Using Microfiber Towels
to Clean Almost Anything with Plain Water

CONTENTS

PREFACE

If someone had told me last year that I would be writing a book about how to clean house, I would have thought that they were completely out of their minds. If anything, I was the "discouraged homemaker"—too busy to keep up; I had just let things go. When I discovered what microfiber towels could do, I was flabbergasted. They cleaned so well—and things stayed clean longer—that I could finally get to those giant dust bunnies that plagued me. If you are a discouraged homemaker, too, please read this book—you're why I wrote it.

CHAPTER 1

Introducing a Super-Green Clean

Microfiber towels can revolutionize the way we all clean house. But this technology doesn't work the way we've cleaned before; instead it uses the principles of physics instead of chemistry. Any homemaker is a pretty fair chemist and knows that "oil and water don't mix" and if you want to clean up grease or oil, you have to use a soap or detergent of some kind. That's the way we've always done it, but that isn't the way it works with microfiber towels.

Microfiber towels *do pick up oil and grease using only water* because they work in a completely different way. But to use them effectively—and be able to clean without chemicals—we have to change our ideas about cleaning. Microfiber towels look a lot like an ordinary cotton terrycloth towel, but there the resemblance ends.

I stumbled upon microfiber towels accidentally and went through a learning period. At first, they seemed to work sometimes and not others. There were no directions for how to clean house with them and I had to learn by trial and error. When I finally figured out *why* microfiber towels work, I found endless uses for them around the house. And, I realized why the house stayed cleaner longer than when I'd been using the conventional cleaning chemicals and methods.

Microfiber technology opens the door for not just a cleaner home, but a cleaner environment as well. They clean using only plain tap water, so you can eliminate many household cleaning chemicals which would otherwise end up in the air or water. They also rinse out with just water. They are reusable and washable, so they won't be adding to the landfill. They pick up extremely fine particles including soot, pollen, dander and dust, so they are a godsend for anyone battling allergies or asthma.

When they first hear about these seemingly miraculous properties, the question that everyone asks is

"Why didn't I know about this?"

The answer that I came to, through my own experiences, is simply that no one has written down the directions for using microfiber towels for house cleaning. This book is really just a beginning guide to help de-mystify microfiber towels. Even though they seem to do the impossible, they aren't "magic."

These towels have been around for quite a few years in computer "clean rooms" and auto detailers have been using them (and raving about them) for cleaning and polishing their prized automobiles. You won't find microfiber towels (yet) in the cleaning aisle at the supermarket, but you can buy them at any auto parts store. Isn't that crazy?

In just a few years, these towels will be part of everyone's regular house cleaning supplies. After only a couple of weeks, I simply couldn't imagine not having them. There will come a day when the younger generation asks, "But, Grandma, how did you ever clean house without microfiber towels?"

CHAPTER 2

Diary of a Convert

I didn't mean to start a revolution—I was just getting my snow tires changed and had a half-hour to kill. I wandered around the showroom, assessing the unliklihood of fancy hubcaps on the minivan. One small display caught my attention. On it were some blue terry cloth towels labeled "the car detailers best friend."

OK, it was something to read. "Microfiber," the label read, "Fast, Easy, Amazing" (uh huh, I've heard that before). But as I read farther: "No Harmful Chemicals, Non-Abrasive...Use on Any Surface...Wash and Reuse 100's of Times."

"Well," I thought, "This could be interesting," and took the package up to the desk to see if I could find out more.

"How much are these?" I asked the gal tending to us pesky customers.

"I don't know," she replied. "I'll have to ask." Obviously, they didn't sell too many of them.

After a few minutes, she returned with the news that the package was fifteen dollars. Yikes, fifteen dollars for just three small towels? Indeed.

I'd started to turn around and take the package back to the display, but being polite, decided to ask, "Have you ever used these?"

"No, I haven't," she replied, "but Tom has." She gestured to a very large, dark-haired man about 30 years old. "This lady is asking about the towels," she explained.

"They are great!" Tom said. "Absolutely great. They get everything clean!"

What? A man raving about a cleaning product? That shocked me. I took another look at the package. "Absorbs Seven Times Its Weight," "Machine Wash and Dry." Hmm.

Well, I brought those towels home and in the afternoon decided to give them a try. The directions were pretty sketchy, but a dust cloth is a dust cloth, isn't it?

(Let me explain here that we live in the country and the county road isn't paved. That means that all summer, every car passing by raises a huge cloud of dust, which drifts over the house. Our local dust is as fine as flour, courtesty of Mt. St. Helen's ash a few years back, and it gets into the house through every nook, cranny, door and window. It also gets tracked in on every boot, tennis shoe and paw. We don't just have dust, we have DUST! It isn't your genteel city dust that waits a week for a house cleaning. It is dust of geologic proportions!)

So, there I was, new dust cloth in hand and re-reading the directions. "For light dusting, use dry." I'd set the cloth on top of the television set (which attracts so much dust that the picture is obscured in a day). When I picked the cloth back up, THERE WAS A CLEAN SPOT!

I'm glad no one was around because I'm pretty sure I stood there just staring at that clean spot long enough that anyone would have begun to wonder—and then I'd have had to explain myself. But I'd never seen any cleaning product work like that. In the little place that the towel had only touched, there just wasn't any dust, it was all stuck to the rag, er, towel. It had begun to dawn on me that this cloth just might be something that deserved respect.

After dusting the television, I moved to the bookshelves, which never get the attention they need until the tops of the books begin to look furry. The cloth worked fabulously. It got dirtier and dirtier while the books got cleaner and cleaner. In fact the books looked cleaner than they had in years. The towel was even picking up the dust from the little creases in the binding and along the edges of the pages.

By this time, I was pretty impressed. I'd used the disposable dusting cloths, but they had never gotten the books as clean as this towel. The towel, however, was looking filthy. I stepped outside to give the cloth a good shaking to get rid of the dust, expecting clouds of our flour-fine dust to fly. Snap! Nothing. Snap again. Still no dust flying. The cloth wouldn't let go of it. Oh great.

So back to the label I went. "To Clean Towel: Machine Wash and Dry." Nuts. I was just getting going. I left the towel on the counter and took the second one out of the bag. The whole living room had gotten dusted faster than ever before and I was ready to tackle the office next. As I worked along, I began to wonder whether I couldn't rinse the dust off the towel instead.

I retrieved filthy towel number one and ran cold water from the kitchen faucet. It took a while to get wet, but the dirt seemed to be washing off. When the towel was soaked through, I wrung it out like a dishcloth. A lot of muddy water went down the drain. The cloth looked cleaner, but not clean. So I tried it again. Better.

Now I had a damp cloth and thought I'd try that. In the living room, I wiped it along the wood wall—clean! Then the painted wall—clean! This was unbelievable. I was getting excited. I tried the woodwork, various pieces of furniture, tables, anything that caught my eye. The damp cloth really left things clean and I hadn't used anything but this magic cloth and water.

In the kitchen with a really dirty cloth, I ran a basin of cold water this time to see what would happen if I swished the cloth around in it. Instant mud. The cloth had let loose of most of the dirt. I drained the sink and refilled it. This time I just dunked the towel, up and down, in and out of the water. With each dunking, the towel released more dirt. This was great. I didn't have to stop. The towel cleaned up with just water.

With each item I cleaned, I was more and more impressed—and I was gaining confidence. I took a clean, damp towel outdoors and called my husband. "Just watch this!" With that one cloth, I washed every one of the dirty windows on my minivan. Even he had to admit I had reason to be babbling, because babbling I was. When I finally stopped for a minute, I asked him, "I sound like an infomercial, don't I?"

He laughed.

By the next morning, I was wondering what else the magic towel was good for and decided to try the internet for cleaning information. Quite a few sites came up with information about microfiber towels—for car cleaning, hair drying and lens cleaning—but nothing for general house cleaning. That was surprising. I was a little hesitant to use it before I really knew what it was good for and what it *shouldn't* be used for.

On the car maintenance web sites, most of the information was very general. The microfiber towels were touted as being able to clean everything on the interior of a car. Everything? Well, that's what they said, *including grease and oil.*

Only one mention on one of the websites indicated that I wasn't a lone convert. The car cleaning cloths had been tested by men and given a glowing recommendation. As an afterthought, the writer mentioned that he had taken one of the cloths home to his wife and she "just raved."

That wasn't much to go on, but I reasoned that there were a lot of different kinds of surfaces in a car—metal, fabric, vinyl, enamel, plastic, cloth, glass, etc. I just figured I'd try the cloth on different things and see how it worked. Over the next few days, I really gave the towel a tryout and it cleaned miraculously sometimes, but not others, and I couldn't figure out why. Slowly, I learned that I had been trying to "help" the towels by using them with cleaners or too much water. In other words, I'd been using it just like any regular cleaning cloth, but the microfiber towels worked on a completely different principle than anything else. Once I figured out what that principle was, I could clean nearly anything: from the greasy stovetop to windows, floors, walls, furniture, etc. Over and over, I was amazed at what a microfiber towel could do with just water. And, over and over, I kept asking myself: *"Why didn't I know about these things?"*

I will admit to some very uncharitable thoughts about the large companies that sell thousands of cleaning products and chemicals each year. I suspected that they were holding out on us, since if everyone started using microfiber towels, they wouldn't sell nearly as much. After my own experiences, though, I changed my mind. I've come to realize that the microfiber towels work so differently than convention cleaning, that even experts in home economics wouldn't know the "how" or "why" of the towels. They would probably do just what I did initially, trying to combine the old way of cleaning with this new product and getting unreliable results. The big companies probably *had* tested these towels and didn't think they were any improvement—or not enough of an improvement—to put on the market for the homemaker.

CHAPTER 3:

A New Way of Thinking About Cleaning

Microfiber towels can clean so much better than soaps or detergents, simply because they use the surface tension of water itself at the microscopic level to clean the absolute surface of just about any material.

Regular cleaning cloths and paper towels work because they are absorbent. They can pick up liquids, but they can only absorb what has been dissolved in the liquid. Soaps and cleaners have to dissolve an oily deposit and then the liquid is absorbed by the towel fibers. However, when you use soap and water in the traditional way, a thin film of water stays on the surface. Even if you rinse with water to remove the soap, that film remains.

If you could see the microscopic view of what is really going on at the surface of your kitchen counter, for example, you would see that the fibers in your cleaning rag or paper towel are relatively large and generally round. They move along pushing the water ahead of them, absorb as much as they can, and then leave a layer of liquid behind. They also leave behind particles that weren't dissolved by the water or cleaner.

Because microfiber towels come in direct contact with the surface, they do not ride on a film of water or leave a film of water behind. (If they do, you're using them too wet.) Since the microfibers are so small, they can directly lift and hold even microscopic particles. The particles that the towel picks up are held inside the fibers and between the fibers—and they stay there until the towel is rinsed in plain water. The result is a tremendously cleaner surface.

For the harried homemaker, that sort of cleaning has a wonderful side effect—*surfaces stay cleaner longer* when they have been cleaned with a microfiber towel. Here's why. The residue left on a surface cleaned with a soap, spray cleaner or detergent actually attracts dust and other tiny particles. When a surface is cleaned with a microfiber towel, there is no residue left, so the dust doesn't accumulate as quickly.

What is a Microfiber?

To understand microfibers you have to think very, very small. Take a look at the handle of a broom. Imagine that the handle represents a human hair. Hold a hair next to the broom handle. That represents a microfiber. That is how small microfibers are—about 1/100th the size of a human hair. Interesting you say, but so what? Well, think about this. In the same space that would be taken up by a cotton thread in a cloth, there are hundreds of microfibers. You may be familiar with fine cotton bed sheets. They brag about having 250, 300 or more threads per inch. In microfiber cloths the fiber count is *90,000 and up*.

The microfibers made for cleaning are made up of two different chemicals: polyester and polyamide. The polyamide is at the center of the microfiber strand and is absorbent (it attracts water). The polyester is around the outside of the fiber, and while it isn't absorbent, it is durable so that it will stand up to rubbing. The round fibers are then "split" into a shape resembling a star or asterisk and the process creates infinitesimally small grooves and channels leading though the polyester to the center of the fiber. Water is

A microfiber is made of two different materials. The absorbent inner part of the fiber and the outer layer of polyester, which is durable.

As small as microfibers are, when they are "split" they contain even smaller channels leading from the outside to the inside of the fiber. The center of the fiber is made of polyamide, which is absorbent and attracts water. A thin film of water fills the channels creating "surface tension." When fine particles are drawn into the channels, the surface tension of the water holds them in place. When the microfiber is submerged in plain water, the surface tension is neutralized and the tiny particles are released by the microfiber.

Because microfiber towels don't ride on a film of water, they can reach the surface of the material to be cleaned and remove particles which don't have to be dissolved in water.

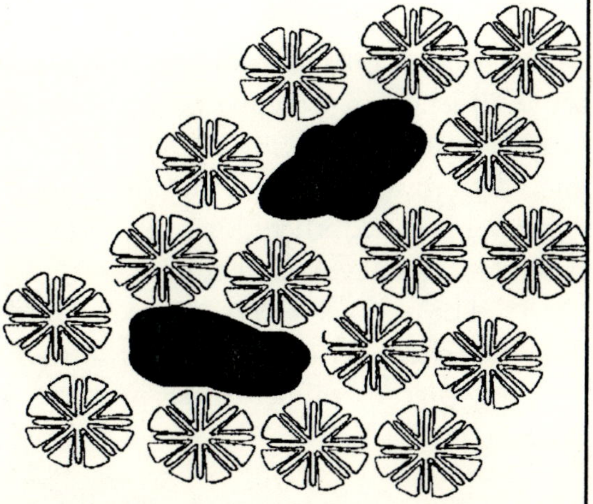

Microfiber towels can also pick up, trap and hold particles that are larger than the fibers themselves. These larger particles are held in place with the surface tension of water between the individual microfibers.

draw into these microscopic channels, bringing the tiniest particles with them. The surface tension of the water itself holds the particles in the towel until it is rinsed.

Larger particles of dirt, oil, grease and sand are held between the strands of microfiber—also by the surface tension of water. Notice in the drawings that the particles, large and small, are held within the towel itself; they aren't riding on the surface of the towel. They can't be re-deposited on the surface.

What makes a microfiber towel remarkable is that *it doesn't care what the particles on the surface are made of.* They can be wax or oil, dust or pollen, bacteria or tiny insects like dust mites. Once the towel has taken hold of the particles, it simply doesn't let go of them until the towel is rinsed. Then all of those particles are released into the rinse water and go down the drain. The whole process uses only *plain tap water.*

Conventional Cleaning vs. Microfiber Cleaning

For generations, we have all been used to using strong cleaners and disinfectants to get surfaces really clean and kill germs. We've all heard that regular sponges and dishrags "just spread the germs around" so chemicals have to be used to kill them. The microfiber towels don't spread germs: they grab and hold them until the towel is rinsed, then down the drain they go. This is a kind of cleaning we've never had before.

The only catch is that there are a few new rules to follow to keep the microfiber towels working as they should. I found out the hard way that microfiber towels just don't work with conventional cleaning methods.

- **Conventional Cleaning: Things rinse out cleaner under running water.** Not microfiber towels. They need to be rinsed in standing water. Just swish them around and dunk them in and out of the water.
- **Conventional Cleaning: A rag will scrub effectively when it is wadded up.** Not microfiber towels. They should be used "open" so that the greatest area of the towel can work on the surface. Also, the little grooves in the microfibers can get filled up with particles, so keep turning the cloth to move to a fresh area as you clean. If a microfiber towel leaves a smear behind it, that means that the towel is fully loaded with grime and needs to be rinsed out.
- **Conventional Cleaning: Soap and hot water are the best things to get things clean.** Not with microfiber towels. Soap and detergents will deactivate the microfibers and really hot water can damage the microfibers. Use only cool to lukewarm water with the towels.
- **Conventional Cleaning: You have to use a cleaner or de-greaser to get heavy grease and oil.** Not with microfiber towels. (I know this sounds like fiction until you've experienced it yourself, but it's true.) Don't use any cleaner or disinfectant with microfiber towels that says on the label that it "cuts grease." That includes disinfectants that use rubbing (isopropyl) alcohol.

CHAPTER 4

Buying the Right Microfiber Towel for Cleaning House

Microfibers are being made of acrylic, nylon, rayon and polyester in various weaves and qualities for very specialized jobs. With so many choices, it would be easy to end up with a towel that doesn't really work well for housecleaning. So, when you go looking for a magic towel of your own, these are the things to note:

- The towel should be made of polyester (75% to 80%) and polyamide (20% to 25%). The polyester forms the wedges at the edges for scrubbing and the polyamide (nylon) is in the center and absorbs water. The first towels I used were 75% polyester and 25% polyamide, but as long as the blend is within the range above, they will do fine for cleaning house.
- The towel should be made of ***split microfibers*** and say so on the label. There are cheap towels that look similar, but the fibers aren't split, so they just won't work for cleaning fine particles. Expect to pay around $5.00 or $6.00 per towel.

- The towel should look like a fine grade of terry cloth on at least one side. The ones I've used look like terry cloth on both sides, but have a little shorter nap on one side. Don't get a waffle weave towel for cleaning. They are for drying things. Avoid towels with long loops in the terry cloth since the thicker towels can't be really wrung out.
- The towel should have a bound or sewn edge that feels soft. Poor quality towels have coarse (rough) threads or a hard cut edge. The auto detailers have to worry about microscopic scratches on their expensive paint jobs, so some manufacturers are making "edgeless" cloths or ones with rounded corners. Those specialty cloths are more expensive, and those features just don't matter for general house cleaning. But, if you are cleaning a delicate, antique porcelain figurine, for example, then it would probably be worth the extra expense for a special towel.
- The towel should have a fiber count of 90,000 or more but a higher count doesn't necessarily mean a better quality or better cleaning ability. The structure of the fiber and the weave are more important. Microfiber towels aren't judged like bed sheets where the higher the thread count the better, but it does make a difference if the count is lower than 90,000 or the terry loops look sparse or uneven.
- The towel should be labeled as able to absorb 7 to 9 times its own weight and should feel soft to the touch. A good microfiber towel will feel a little weird when you first handle one. Even dry, the electrostatic attraction of the fibers will make it feel "clingy"—as if it wants to hold onto your skin and cling to itself.
- Some microfiber towels are labeled "lint free." That basically means that they were treated at the factory to remove the lint that collected during manufacturing. It doesn't mean that they won't shed lint—microfiber towels won't do that anyway. I've tried both types, and they work exactly the same for cleaning. The only difference is that the first time you rinse a towel that isn't lint free, the rinse water will look milky as the towel is releasing the lint on its surface.

That seems like a lot to remember, but if you're at an auto supply store, look for the general purpose cleaning towels for auto detailing. At the back of the book are some of the suppliers that I found on the internet and I'm sure there are more. At every automobile-related business that we've checked, there are microfiber towels available.

As of this writing, a good cleaning towel is $5.00 to $6.00 from reliable suppliers. Towels are offered individually, but the 3-packs or 5-packs are a better buy and you'll want more than one towel. It didn't take long for me to find out that one towel should live in the office, one in the kitchen and one in the car.

Microfiber towels are offered in a variety of sizes, but I found the 16-inch square size practical for just about everything. You don't want a towel that is so large that it is a problem to wring out.

There are cheap, poor quality towels showing up at flea markets, big box discount stores and internet auctions. Be cautious of those, even when they are labeled "microfiber" and/or "top quality" if they don't give the important details above. The worst part of the cheap towels is that their fibers aren't even split into the star pattern (which costs money to do, of course). Instead their microfibers are round and just don't pick up the dirt, grime and fine particles like the good towels do. I can just hear someone saying "I tried cleaning with a microfiber towel and it didn't do any better than my regular cloth." Not everything that says "microfiber" on it is a good cleaning cloth.

If you're put off by the idea of spending $5.00 or $6.00 for a cloth, do the same sort of calculation that I did. Look at how much you have spent for paper towels, disposable dusting cloths, glass cleaners and surface cleaners in the last month. Just in the last month. Remember that a good microfiber towel can be rinsed and reused over and over again—and do the same cleaning job better. Then add in the environmental costs of the paper towels and plastic cleaner bottles as they fill up landfills. Finally, look at the labels on the cleaning products you use around the house. Those chemicals end up in our air and water.

If you have children with allergies or asthma, you don't even have to go through that calculation. I found one website which mentioned how good microfiber towels were at picking up dust and pollen and recommended them for preventing allergies (but they didn't include any instructions for using them). In the meantime, $5.00 is unbelievably cheap to anyone who needs help fighting the allergy battle.

One more point that I have to bring up is that I found two references to a study which reportedly revealed that wiping down surfaces with a damp microfiber towel removed more than 99% of the surface bacteria. No one seems to be able to cite the source for that claim, but a good quality microfiber towel works with extremely small particles—even smaller than a bacterium—and once I figured out the physics of why microfibers work, it was obvious that they would pick up bacteria. I tested the rinse water myself and sure enough, there were lots of bacteria. What I couldn't test was how clean the surface was. I'm sure there will be lots of studies before too long, but when you really need to fight germs, you can add disinfectant to the water that you rinse the towel in for extra insurance.

CHAPTER 5

Cleaning with, and Caring for a Microfiber Towel

The very first time I used a microfiber towel, I used it dry like a regular dust cloth. Of course, I've learned that the towels work best when they are damp, but because of the extremely small openings in the microfiber grooves, you have to *"wake up"* a towel being used for the very first time. With a new towel, you want to wet it down thoroughly and then ***really wring it out***, at least twice, to make sure that the moisture gets all the way into the fibers. Don't try to wet it under running water from the faucet. Instead, fill a sink, basin or bucket with plain water (cool to lukewarm) and hold the towel underwater for several seconds before you wring it out. Once it starts to hold water, dunk it in and out of the water several times before you wring it out. Do that at least twice to allow the wicking action of the fibers to get established. After rinsing, towels need to be wrung out completely, as dry as you can get them. Then start dusting or cleaning as usual.

Since it takes a little time for water to work its way into the microfibers, you will notice that it cleans even better after a few minutes. I've learned to let a newly-wetted towel rest for a few minutes to allow time for the water to get distributed.

If you have your very first towel and are reading these directions—put the book down and just go try the cloth out on a wall or table or television set; any hard surface will do. Just play around with it awhile. If the towel is leaving streaks behind when you wipe, it has too much water at the surface. Wring it out again or let it rest a few minutes so that the water can be absorbed into the microfibers.

For the best cleaning, the towel should feel just barely damp. Keep turning the towel as you dust or clean. The microfibers will pick up so much—especially the first time you clean a surface with one—that the little grooves can get filled to the point where they just can't pick up any more.

When towel starts looking dirty, run a sink full of cool to lukewarm water and dunk the towel several times. Just put the towel in the water and, holding the edges, lift it out. With each dunking, the towel will be cleaner because water—**plain tap water**—releases the particles that are held in the microfiber. If the water gets really dirty, drain the sink and refill it again with cool water. I was astonished at *how much* dirt the cloth picked up, and at how readily the dirt and grime rinsed out without using any soap at all.

When the towel is rinsed, wring it out well again and continue using it. If you're cleaning very greasy, oily or waxy areas, add a drop of dishwashing soap *(one drop)* to the rinse water *after* you've rinsed the towel. When you rinse out an oily cloth, take a look at the surface of the water. The oil (or wax) will be floating on the top. Too much grease can clog plumbing lines, so just a drop of dishwashing liquid is all that is needed to dissolve the greasy stuff and protect your pipes.

I've learned not to worry that a microfiber towel doesn't rinse perfectly clean. It won't look "new" after rinsing. Instead, I've learned to watch the rinse water. When the towel has stopped releasing more dirt into the rinse water, it is fine to use for more cleaning. So though the towel will still look "dingy" keep using it. It only needs to be washed when it really looks dirty.

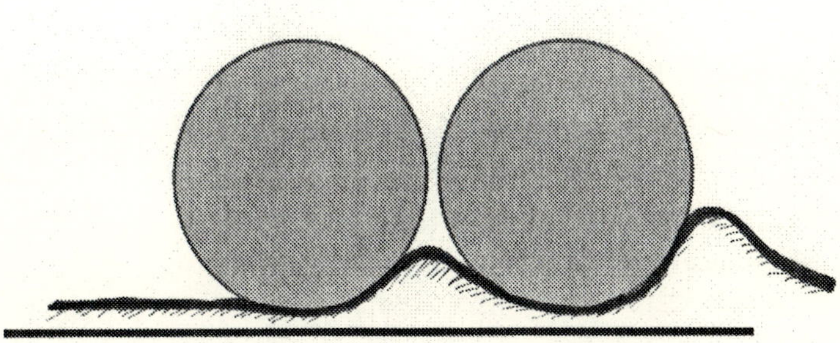

With conventional cleaning, the large rounded fibers of a cotton cloth or paper towel work by absorbing the liquid (either soap and water or a liquid cleaner). The fine film of water, which is left behind from conventional cleaning contains small particles that can't be dissolved, and this residue can actually attract more dust to the surface.

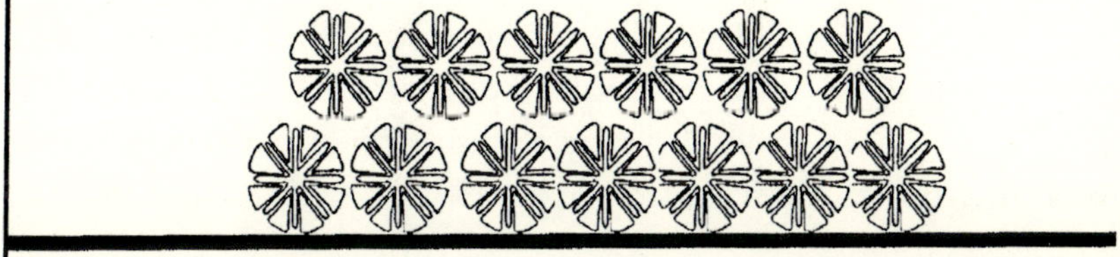

In contrast microfiber towels reach to the surface of the material itself, and remove even the residue left by conventional cleaning. Microfibers can clean any smooth surface, and are so small that they can reach an irregular or textured surface too.

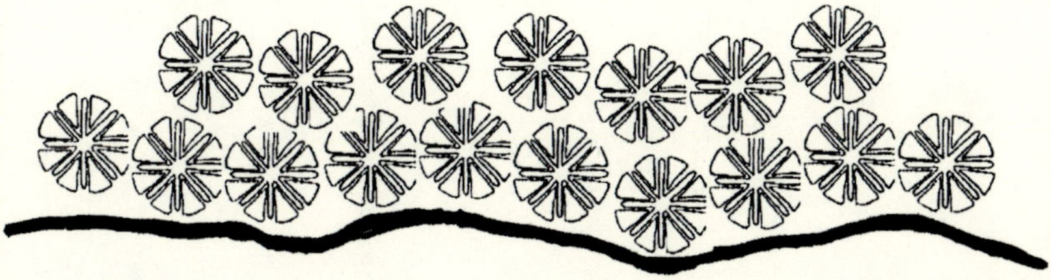

NOTE: Microfiber towels by themselves won't scratch glass or delicate surfaces. But they are very good at picking up grit (particles of dirt or sand). If you have grit in the towel and wash a window, you stand the chance of scratching it. So if you're going to clean windows, glass objects or other delicate surfaces, make sure to use a freshly clean, well-rinsed towel. (See the Chapter 14 for more information about cleaning windows.)

When you're done cleaning for the day, rinse the towel again before you put it in the laundry basket. If you don't, all of the dirt and oils will come out in the washing machine, and you really don't want your other clothes exposed to that.

Microfiber towels can mildew if they are left around wet, just like a dishcloth, and for the same reason. The organic particles that are caught in the fibers are a good medium for mildew to grow. So if you think you'll want to use the same cloth again before you have time to run a load of wash, hang it up to dry completely. As a test, I used one towel for six days running. It worked fine and didn't get sour as long as it had a chance to dry out overnight. If you live in a damp climate, the towel may not air-dry. You can toss a well-rinsed microfiber towel directly in the dryer on the cool or delicate setting.

General Guidelines for Cleaning with Microfiber Towels

In the chapters that follow are some of my experiences in cleaning surfaces around the house. You'll want to experiment with other items, too, so below is a general guide for how the towels work. The microfiber towels will do different jobs with varying amounts of water.

- **DRY:** Use a dry towel for dusting off papers and similar materials that you don't want exposed to moisture. Even dry, the microfiber towels will pick up a lot of surface dust, but they aren't as efficient at actually cleaning the surface as when used with water.
- **MISTED WITH WATER:** Use a misting bottle to just spray the surface of the microfiber towel. The towel can then be used to pick up light surface dust from delicate textiles (use a blotting action, not a rubbing action).
- **DAMP—WET AND REALLY WRUNG OUT:** This is how you want to use the towels for just about everything. It takes wetting the microfibers for them to be the most efficient, but the towel doesn't need to get a surface wet to get it clean.
- **LIGHTLY WET:** This is what I would refer to as "dishrag wet"—it isn't wrung completely out, but it isn't dripping water either. The towel won't pick up particles quite as efficiently (but still remarkably well compared to conventional cleaners). Use this level of wetness when you are using a disinfectant in the water and want to leave some of it on the surface.
- **SOPPING WET:** Don't expect a microfiber towel to work when it is sopping wet or underwater. When the towels are saturated with water, the microfibers are de-activated, which is why they will rinse clean in plain water. Sopping wet, a microfiber towel isn't any better than a plain cotton cloth.

When Conventional Cleaning Methods Work Better than Microfiber Towels

Microfiber technology can do an amazing number of cleaning jobs, but you can't throw out your vacuum cleaner just yet. And the laundry and dishes will still have to be washed. There are a few other instances that I found when conventional cleaning methods work better than microfiber towels.

- If you have a really large wet spill, paper towels or sponges will work better at absorbing the liquid. Microfiber towels (either dry or damp) will absorb about a cup of liquid (8 oz.). So they can be used for a glass of spilled milk or juice. But, for larger spills, I think it is a little more efficient to use other tools and just finish up with a microfiber towel to pick up any residue.
- If a substance is physically attached to the surface, like burned on food, scrubbing with a microfiber towel will take a long time to remove it. Instead, use a cleaner, or soak it in soap and water to get the worst of it up. Then you can get the surface itself really clean with a microfiber towel.
- Heavy, sticky spills, like a glob of jelly or honey is best wiped up first with a wet paper towel. Then the microfiber towel can be used to get any sticky residue off.
- Microfiber towels can only clean what they can touch. If a stain has actually penetrated the surface of a fabric or countertop, the microfibers can't remove it. Instead, use a suitable stain remover.
- Porous surfaces, like clay pots, grout, foam rubber, etc., have deep irregularities that the microfiber can't reach. For those, a liquid cleaner is better.

Machine Washing a Microfiber Towel

The only directions that came with my first microfiber towels said "Machine wash and dry." Very guy-like directions, I thought, and as I found out later, *a good way to ruin a microfiber towel.* I found out that the towels really don't need to be machine washed as often as I'd first thought. Towels can be used all week, and then put through a wash—if they are rinsed out every night and spread out or hung to dry. If the towel has gotten really filthy, you can even hand-wash them in lukewarm water using a liquid dishwashing or laundry detergent. After washing, rinse thoroughly to remove the soap completely.

Basic Directions for Machine Washing:

- **NEVER** use hot water with a microfiber towel; the fibers will shrink and not work as well (the tiny channels close up). This means cool to lukewarm water to rinse the towel with as you're working, and the "cool" or "cold" setting on the washing machine.
- **NEVER** expose the microfiber towel to heat. Use the coolest ("delicate") setting on the dryer, don't iron it (why would anyone?) and don't use it on hot objects. With high temperatures the synthetic fibers will melt.
- **NEVER** use a fabric softener with a microfiber towel. Not in the washer and not in the dryer. The chemicals in the softeners will coat the microfibers, keeping them from working like they should.
- **NEVER** wash a microfiber towel with regular terry cloth towels, socks or other items that shed a lot of lint. The microfiber towel will pick up the lint from cotton towels and get clogged up. Instead, wash the microfiber towels in a load with other fabrics that also need cool water. If you do put a microfiber towel in the wrong wash load, and it is covered in lint, soak and rinse it several times to get the lint out before you use it for cleaning. What I have learned is that the towels actually wash up the best if you do a load of just the microfiber towels. They need lots of

water, so only put about half as many in the wash as you would with regular fabrics. I tested a load just going through the rinse cycle with four towels, and they were just about as clean as the ones that had gone through the wash cycle too.

- **NEVER** use powdered cleansers with a microfiber towel. The towel will *pick up* the grit in the cleaner so it doesn't work on the surface.
- **NEVER** let wet paint, glazes, glues or milk dry on the surface of a microfiber towel. They can attach permanently to the fibers. If you can't rinse out the towel right away, drop it in a basin of water to soak in the meantime.
- **AVOID** powdered laundry products since some of them don't dissolve all of the way and grains of the detergent will get picked up by the microfibers. The same is true if you want to use a disinfectant with the towel—stick to the liquids. You can add bleach to the wash load, but only use about half as much as you would for bleaching whites. (The exact amount will depend on how large your washing machine is.)
- **ALWAYS** rinse out the towel after use so that it doesn't carry a lot of dirt into the washing machine with it, and so that it doesn't mildew.

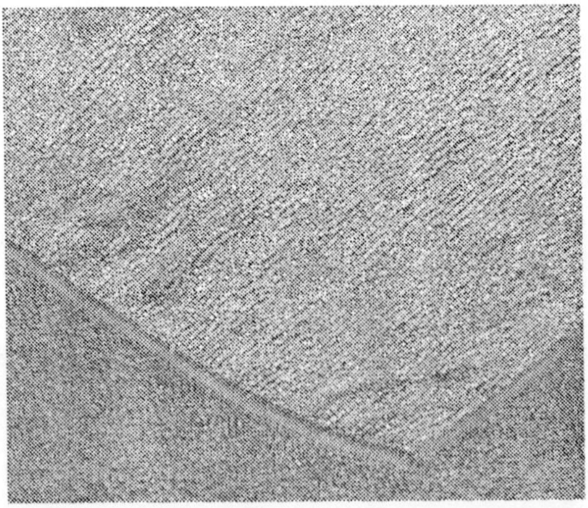

A typical microfiber cleaning towel. Notice the shorter nap shown on top, and the longer nap on the back side.

Real Life with a Microfiber Towel

Above are the "standard" directions for caring for a microfiber towel, but I've learned that microfiber towels are actually easier to care for than the directions make it look. The towels can be used and rinsed out all week (or longer) without washing—just make sure to hang them up to dry overnight. They can be hung on the drainboard, a towel rack or outdoors over a rail or clothesline.

To get the towels the cleanest, and preserve their fibers, about once a week run a wash load with only the towels in it. They really don't need added laundry detergent at all unless they've been used with lots of heavy waxes, grease or oils. (At most add only about a tablespoon of liquid laundry detergent to the load.) When they come out of the final spin cycle, they are at a perfect dampness to use, so I don't usually even put them in the dryer.

Microfiber towels aren't fragile. When I first began using them, I wasn't sure how careful I should be with them. It turns out that they are real workshorses and stand up to quite a lot of use and heavy scrubbing. If you remember the days of the polyester pant suits that wouldn't wear out, you have a good idea of the durability of microfiber towels. I'm afraid that it didn't take me long to start taking them for granted!

When Microfiber Towels Clean *Too* Well!

Microfiber towels can do too good a job of cleaning some things. Remember they don't care what a particle is made of, they will pick it up off a surface anyway. Most of the time that is just what you want when you're cleaning, but sometimes it isn't.

For example, if you have a decorative item with a painted-on design, a damp microfiber towel will take off any paint that isn't bonded or sealed to the surface. So only use the dry towel for dusting tole painted items, ceramics with only surface painted designs, painted tins and, of course paintings themselves.

In the general directions for using the microfiber towels, I noted that only dry towels should be used for dusting papers. There is an important reason for that. A damp microfiber towel will lift the ink right off the page of some books, magazines, cards, etc. The damp towel will take off any printing that isn't bonded to the base paper itself. Anything that was printed with an off-set press is vulnerable, and inks that stand up above the surface in textures will come off too.

Use only a dry microfiber towel to dust the surfaces of:

- Papers
- Books
- Magazines
- Photographs, photo negatives and slide film
- Paper memorabilia including greeting cards

If there is any question in your mind whether the ink on a printed item is only on the surface (not bonded to it), just don't risk using a damp microfiber towel.

CHAPTER 6

Cleaning Furniture

Wood Furniture

Wood furniture can be dusted, cleaned and polished with a damp microfiber towel since the towel really doesn't wet down the surface. Just remember to really wring out the towel before you start. Use the side of the towel with the longer nap for getting into the tiny grooves and corners. If you've been using furniture polish or a dusting spray, you'll find out that the microfiber towels really do a better job for regular cleaning, and the short-nap side of the towel brings up an excellent shine. If the wood on the furniture is very dry and you want to apply an oil or polish to it, *don't use the microfiber cloth to do that job*. Instead, apply the furniture oil or polish with a regular cloth or paper towel and let it dry completely. Then use the microfiber cloth to remove any excess and do the polishing.

My antique treadle sewing machine has an elaborately carved wooden cabinet. I hadn't been able to get to all of the little details before without resorting to a cotton swab dipped in a cleaner. I was delighted with the performance of the damp microfiber towel at reaching into the nooks and crannies and really getting them clean.

With that much detail (and how much grime had collected over 80 years) I did have to work with the cloth to get to all of the little spaces, but it was sure a lot easier than the way I had been doing it and the cabinet looked much cleaner afterward.

With smooth wooden surfaces, just wipe with the microfiber towel. If the furniture has a high polish on it, keep in mind the warning about grit in the previous chapter. The microfiber towels won't scratch the finish, but if they have been used to clean a really dirty surface, they will hold onto the grit and the grit can scratch the finish. So make sure that the microfiber towel is rinsed clean before working on a highly polished surface.

Painted wood furniture also comes really clean with a microfiber towel. I was surprised to see a shine on some old painted chests after the surface had been cleaned a couple of times with a damp towel. Those chests had never had a shine before.

Combined Glass and Wood Furniture

One of the peskiest furniture cleaning problems is wood cabinets with glass panels. The furniture polish used on the wood gunks up the glass, and glass cleaners can dry out and damage the wood. I fell in love with microfiber towels the first time I tackled that problem. The damp microfiber towel cleaned (and polished) the wood frame and even got down into the grooves, removing the built up grime. I turned the same towel over and cleaned the glass panel next to the wood. Both shone like new. Having a little more experience with microfiber towels now, I can recommend using the side of the towel with the shorter nap on the glass, and the longer nap on the wood. That extra little bit of nap really gets down in the grooves of the wood trim. If the towel leaves tiny droplets of water on the glass, wipe them off with a paper towel.

The same technique works wonderfully on wooden picture frames—especially if there is a lot of detailed carving where old polish has accumulated. Another application where microfiber towels are a real improvement is in cleaning display cases made of wood and glass. I have a friend who has several treasured antique dolls that are in those cases. She has a terrible time with cleaning them because the chemicals in glass cleaners and furniture cleaners can both damage the fragile old fibers in the doll costumes. With a microfiber towel—problem solved. She can clean the entire display case, inside and out, using plain water.

Vinyl and Other Plastics in Furniture

If you have tried to clean vinyl or other plastic furniture, you know how those materials will hold onto dirt, particularly oily dirt. That can get to be a real problem especially if you have kids. A damp microfiber towel will get the furniture really clean with no cleaning chemicals needed. For grime of long standing, you'll have to scrub some. The biggest test with the vinyl furniture was the "leather look" deep textured seats and backs of our office chairs. The microfiber cloth got into those little depressions and seams beautifully and the chairs looked new.

The plastic outdoor furniture had a smooth surface and it was a snap just to wipe it clean. Wood laminate furniture cleans up with just wiping with a damp microfiber towel. Like all plastics, it seems to attract the oily sort of dirt (grimy fingerprints and such) so it was great to have that come right up without scrubbing or chemicals.

Leather Furniture

Leather furniture is very popular and the pieces come with pretty detailed cleaning instructions. Microfiber towels really solve that problem neatly. The damp towel reaches into the texture of the leather to grab any dirt or dust. Even where there are tufts or seams the dust comes up. The test piece I tried looked so clean it almost looked new. (Even a microfiber towel can't fix the worn places!)

If you have furniture with a rough-out texture (like suede) the microfiber can lift off the surface dust, but it can't get at any stains or oils that have penetrated the leather itself. Rough-out leathers are absorbent and can draw stains below the surface where a microfiber towel just can't reach them.

Metal Furniture

Painted metal can be just wiped clean but chrome finishes on metal need to be handled the same way as glass to avoid scratching the surface. Be sure that the microfiber towel is clean and not carrying along any grit before you clean the surface. Use the side with the longer nap to do any heavy cleaning and finish up with the side with the shorter nap to bring out the shine.

Doorknobs, cabinet hardware and other metal details on furniture are handled the same way. Just a damp cloth is used. If the surface isn't shiny just wipe it clean. If the surface is shiny, use the shorter nap for a quick polishing once it's clean.

Wicker and Basket Style Furniture

With all of the dust that we have, I generally have avoided wicker and basket furniture just because it is so hard to clean in all of the crevasses between the wicker. We do have a couple of wicker decorative items, so I tried the microfiber cloth on them. The damp microfiber towel did do better than a regular damp cloth or a disposable dusting cloth, but it still couldn't reach way down in to get at the deep places. I'd had hopes, but maybe someone will invent a microfiber product that can get wicker clean in the tiny spaces.

Upholstered Furniture

It was a big surprise to me that the microfiber towel would clean upholstery. If you have synthetic plush-type upholstery, rub back and forth with the towel to start. You want the towel to touch as many upholstery fibers as possible. We have one chair with a plush, velveteen surface and lots of creases where the back is button-tufted. It collects dust like mad, and the vacuum never quite gets everything out of the button areas. I tried a damp microfiber cloth and it worked. The tufts were clean. It did take some work getting between the folds of the fabrics, but the whole area looked clean for a change. The cloth also picked up a muddy pawprint that had (somehow) gotten on the arm of the chair.

With woven upholstery fabrics a circular motion with the cloth seems to work best. I tried both wool and synthetic upholstered pieces and they were much cleaner than when they were just vacuumed. You shouldn't be "scrubbing" with the towel, especially on delicate fabrics. The microfiber towel only needs to come in contact with the surface.

The cloth didn't pick up the pet hair off upholstery, since those fibers are too large for the towel to grab onto. But rubbing with the cloth in just one direction bunched up the hair so that I could just pick it up all at once.

Of course, if your upholstery has a stain, the towel won't be able to reach it, but it will pick up the surface dust and tiny particles. Microfiber towels also won't replace occasional vacuuming of upholstered furniture since they can't reach to any dust that has gotten below the surface.

CHAPTER 7

Cleaning Walls and Ceilings

I hadn't really been aware of how many different types of wall surfaces are in our home—nor how many different cleaners I'd been using for them. Walls are something that I really don't like to clean, especially our walls of oiled tongue-in-groove cedar. But because we use wood heat in the winter, there is a coating of grime that builds up on all of the walls and ceilings by spring. Even with liquid cleaners, washing them down required a lot of elbow grease, and some places always looked better than others.

Painted Walls

With the gloss and semi-gloss painted walls, the damp microfiber towel was simply a breeze. The walls wiped very clean, even the greasy splatters in the kitchen. With high gloss walls and wood work, the shine was noticeably brighter. With the flat painted walls though, more scrubbing was necessary to get a good cleaning (I had to do some areas twice). What I finally figured out with the flat walls was that the towel was picking up enough dirt from the surface that the center of the towel had gotten dirtier than it should. When I began turning the towel regularly and rinsing the towel more often, it cleaned much better.

A great time-saver is using the damp microfiber towels to clean wall surfaces before repainting. Every can of paint has the same directions it seems. The surface is supposed to be "free of dust and oil." In the past, that meant using a cleaner with water to wash the walls and then wiping them down with water. With the microfiber towel, the wall was ready for repainting with just one pass.

Wallpaper

The vinyl-coated wallpaper was very easy to clean. Just wiping with the damp microfiber towel cleaned and brightened it up. One of the wallpapers was heavily textured and the cloth cleaned it just as well. With paper towels and the liquid cleaner I had been using, that wallpaper had needed a lot of scrubbing to get down into the texture.

We have one area with a cloth face that isn't coated and has always been a problem. Previously, I'd been vacuuming that wall as if it were upholstery. I tried a side by side comparison with the vacuum and the microfiber towel, dry and then slightly dampened. I didn't rub hard with the towel, just "stroked" the surface. The vacuumed area and the area cleaned with the dry towel were about the same. The area I cleaned with the dampened towel was noticeably cleaner. If you have a heavily-textured wallpaper, made of grasses or cloth fibers, the same technique should work fine, but test a small hidden area first.

Polished Wood Walls and Panelling

The areas of polished wood and wood paneling I had been using all sorts of various cleaners, oils, oil soaps and polishes over the years to keep up the shine. They all worked pretty well, but I noticed that there was some grime that had built up in the small crevasses. I used a damp microfiber towel and the side with the longer nap and got a much better cleaning, even in the grooves and crevasses. Then I wiped the flat areas a second time with the side of the towel having the shorter nap. The shine was excellent and the wood hadn't gotten wetted.

Keep in mind the same precaution about using a clean microfiber towel to work on polished wood. The towel itself won't scratch the finish, but if the towel is dirty and gritty, the grit itself can scratch.

Rough Wood Walls

We have several cedar tongue-in-groove walls with a tung oil finish. They don't have a polished surface and they do have lots of irregularities, knots, grooves and rough edges. They are supposed to give a rustic look and they do. For years, I tried cleaners with cotton cleaning rags and the whole process was a giant nuisance. The cotton would catch on the rough places and the grooves never seemed to get entirely clean. When the disposable dusting cloths came along, I'd hoped they would do better, but the rough places on the wood actually ripped the fibers right out of the cloths and I'd have to pick fibers out of the wall. Vacuuming worked for the loose dust but the walls just didn't come really clean. So you can understand that I had high hopes for the microfiber towels on these walls.

The damp microfiber towel vastly exceeded my expectations. Not only did it clean the wood—getting into all of the small irregularities—it didn't catch on the rough places. The cedar looked as good as it had the day it was finished. I had to call my husband again, "You've got to see this!" for about the seventh or eighth time. He actually was the most impressed since he'd tried to clean those walls too.

Ceramic Tile Walls and Mosaics

The one wall which I positively dread the most in spring cleaning is a floor-to-ceiling ceramic tile mosaic which is behind our wood burning stove. It collects dust, of course, but also the grime from the smoke that gets into the room sometimes. Previously, I had used a scrub brush and a pail of water with sudsy ammonia in it to clean the wall, and then washed it down with a cotton rag and plain water. I couldn't wait to see what a microfiber towel would do.

The tile surfaces cleaned up perfectly with just wiping with a damp microfiber towel, and they were squeaky clean. Unfortunately the grout in between didn't come out quite as well. I tried using a dry scrub brush first to loosen up the dust on the grout, then wiping with the microfiber and that was some improvement. The grout surface was simply too porous for the towel to reach into.

On the standard ceramic walls (square tiles with narrow lines of grout), the microfiber towel by itself did much better. Those walls get washed regularly, instead of just once a year like the mosaic wall, so they were probably cleaner to start with. The real difference, I think, is that there is just so much more grout exposed in the mosaic and that is what the microfiber cloth just couldn't reach to get clean.

Ceilings

It seems that most ceilings are painted and ours are with a semi-gloss paint. The microfiber towels did very well in dusting and cleaning, but I'm not tall and climbing up and down a step stool or ladder isn't my idea of fun. I tried a couple of tools with the microfiber towels that did make the job easier. The little mops that are sold for use with the disposable dust cloths have little pockets that the cloths are tucked into. The microfiber towels are much bulkier, but you can tuck just the corners into the pockets and have the cloth itself loosely held. That worked pretty well, except in the corners.

The other tool I tried was from a paint store and they called it a "pad painter." It is a long pole, with a flat metal plate on the end that swivels around. Basically, it resembles the dust-cloth mops but is heavier and sturdier. The towel attaches to the plate with little clamps and is held more securely. If you have to really clean (not just dust) a ceiling, that tool worked better.

CHAPTER 8

Cleaning Floors

Cleaning floors is where a microfiber towel can really save a lot of time, and if you have real wood floors, it can help protect the finish. I noticed on a janitorial supply website that a "mop" was being sold with a microfiber pad, much like the mops sold with the disposable dust cloths. From what I've tried, I think a towel is really a better choice.

If you have an old-fashioned string-mop handle, a folded towel can be attached to it. That way the mop can also be rinsed and wrung out in a mop bucket that has a wringer on it. Otherwise, just lay the damp towel on the floor and push it around with a sponge mop. Work back and forth, just like a regular mop, occasionally repositioning the mop on the towel. The floors I tried, mopped clean—and I mean squeaky clean. On places that needed a bit of a scrub (spills and splatters on the kitchen floor), the mop made it easy to apply a little pressure and the spots came right up.

Floors are where grit tends to collect and the microfiber towel picked it right up of course. But, grit in the towel can mar a delicate surface, so it is important to keep the towel rinsed. We don't have huge rooms, so I just rinsed and wrung out the towel after each room was mopped and that worked very well.

As long as you keep the grit from collecting in the towel, the microfiber can be used for any hard-surface floor. Particularly, if you have real wood floors where tracked in dirt (or worse, sand) can damage the finish, the microfiber towels are a major improvement over the disposable dust cloths for cleaning. The disposables seem to do well with light dust, but I've noticed that they don't pick up the larger sand particles. The microfiber towels will grab and trap the sand and really clean the floor surface at the same time, not just dust it.

The vinyl flooring came cleaner with the microfiber towel than with regular wet mopping—even supplemented by drying with a towel. One nice feature of the microfiber towels is that they are used just barely damp, so there isn't any waiting around for a freshly mopped floor to dry.

Carpeting is another matter of course, so your vacuum cleaner is still needed, but I did try a damp microfiber towel for spot cleaning on one of those mystery spots that show up which, of course, no one mentioned. The rug has a plush surface and short pile. Rubbing with the microfiber towel picked up the stain, but it took a fair amount of rubbing—and then the spot looked cleaner than the rest of the rug. Oh, well.

CHAPTER 9:

Around the Office

One of the first places I tried out a microfiber towel was in our home office. The electronic adding machine has been an absolute nuisance to clean because of the dust that collects between the keys. When I saw how well the towel worked—and without a lot of fuss—I was sold. If you have computers, copiers, fax machines, telephones, etc., you know exactly what I mean. The plastic that is used on the cases and keys seems to be a magnet for body oil and grimy fingerprints show up all of the time. I used just the damp microfiber towel on everything and was delighted with the results.

After really cleaning the surfaces with a damp microfiber towel, I found that it was handy to keep a dry towel in the office for any light dust that showed up. All of the surfaces have stayed much cleaner, and the dry towel is fine for just keeping it clean with a quick swipe.

Telephones

Use the side of the towel with the longer nap, and just wipe thoroughly. We have telephones in white, black and ivory and they all looked new after cleaning. The only part that the towel couldn't get to was inside the little holes in the plastic of the earpiece on an old hand set.

Computer Monitors and Other Glass

Make sure before cleaning the glass surfaces that the microfiber towel is clean. Computer monitors attract a lot of dust since they act like an electro-static magnet—just like a television. The microfiber towel picked up the dust and cleaned the surface very well, but I did do a final drying with a paper towel just for insurance. If you have to look at a screen for extended periods, a spot or streak of any kind just adds to the eyestrain.

I also used the towel on the glass plate of the scanner and copier and the plastic screen covers on several other pieces of equipment. What I *didn't* use it on was the lens of the digital camera. That type of glass (as well as most eyeglasses) has a very delicate coating on the surface. There is a very fine type of microfiber that is sold just for lens cleaning and you should stick to those for cleaning optics of any sort. Places that sell eyeglasses have the optical grade cloths and they are also available on the internet.

I had always been a little afraid of damaging the display screen on the laptop computer in trying to clean it. Since I often work with it outdoors, it had gathered a lot of tiny specks of tree sap, which just wouldn't come off, even with rubbing alcohol (which only seemed to smear the specks and make the situation worse). The damp microfiber towel cleaned the sap spots right up and the monitor looked new again.

Plastic Surfaces

The plastic used in the cabinets that electronics come in is of a special type, which is good for the electronics but has a real talent for attracting body oils, so dirty fingerprints show up quickly. The microfiber towels are great for picking up the fingerprints as well as dust. Before you begin to wipe down the electronics though, make sure they are *turned off!*

The plastic cases can be cleaned with just wiping. Use the side of the towel with the longer nap for textured surfaces and the shorter nap for shiny surfaces. Around any connections, be particularly cautious. Many of the connections for computers have special metallic pins that should not be touched by anything, and that includes a microfiber towel. On the back of computers (where most cables connect) leave the connected cables and wires plugged and delicately blot with the towel around them to pick off the dust without disturbing the connection.

Computer keyboards are another big problem area, and one thing I have learned over the years is to turn the keyboard *upside-down* before you begin to dust it with anything! Dust particles can get down in the keyboard and mess up the connections. Over the years I've tried the air dusters, miniature "computer vacuums" and the disposable dust cloths for the dusting. To clean the surfaces and between the keys, I'd used a cotton swab dipped in rubbing alcohol. A damp microfiber cloth worked very well for the dusting step (upside-down), working back and forth across the keys and the flat surfaces between. Then with the keyboard right-side-up, I folded the microfiber towel so that it could fit better between the keys. It worked very well and there were only a couple of tiny places that I had to resort to the cotton swab and rubbing alcohol.

Papers and Books

Have I mentioned that we have a huge amount of dust? One of the worst problems is keeping exposed papers on the desk from getting dirty. It was in cleaning the papers that I'd been "hooked" on the disposable dusting cloths. Their fibers are electrostatically charged so they could be used on surfaces that couldn't get wet (like paper). The *dry* microfiber towel worked as well or better.

The dry microfiber cloth also worked for dusting books, both the pages and the covers. However, I have quite a number of cookbooks (hardback) that have been exposed to the moisture, oils and smoke that a kitchen generates as well as the dust. I tried the damp microfiber towel on the covers and they looked much cleaner. Not perfect or "new"—but a big improvement. The covers I tried included cloth, coated cloth and leather bindings (which cleaned up the best).

I also tried the damp microfiber cloth on some of our old encyclopedias and they looked a lot better. If you have antique or fragile books, I wouldn't risk the damp cloth on the bindings, but in the types of hardbacks that I worked on the microfiber towel did a much better job on the bindings than any dry cloth or duster has.

CD's and DVD's

These disks are delicate and the surfaces can be damaged by fine scratches, but they seem to collect a lot of fingerprints—especially if children are handling them a lot. You can clean the disks with a microfiber cleaning towel that is damp, but only if the microfiber towel is perfectly clean. The same cautions should be used as when cleaning glass. I've designated one towel that just lives in the office so that it can be used on these delicate surfaces and I don't use it anywhere else. You might want to consider a special glass cleaning microfiber towel if you have a lot of disks to keep clean.

Other Surfaces

In our home office there are lots of other surfaces from wood and laminate to metals in the various furniture pieces. See the chapter on cleaning furniture for those. The only other "odd" surface that was in the office was a cork bulletin board of indeterminate age. The cork never got much cleaning attention since it was usually covered up with papers, but the damp microfiber towel got it looking surprisingly good.

CHAPTER 10

In the Kitchen

The kitchen seems to be the room that requires the most cleaning time. It not only has the dust and dirt that other rooms get, but humidity, smoke, oil, sticky substances, grease and other sorts of lovely things that collect on surfaces. There are spills, splatters and blobs dropped that attach to a lot of different types of surface finishes, so I was really interested to see how the microfiber towel would function.

Remember to use a clean towel—free of grit—to clean and polish shiny surfaces. Either side of the towel can be used for general cleaning in the kitchen, but for a high-gloss polish use the side with the shorter nap.

Appliances

On the first day I had a towel, I tried wiping the refrigerator and was thrilled with how clean it was, and shiny. Enamel surfaces on appliances are really easy. Just a clean, damp towel and wipe them down. Most kitchen appliances collect an oily residue from cooking, so you'll need a drop—not more—of dishwashing liquid in the water you've rinsed the towel in. Especially stove tops can get a lot of grease splatters, so keep turning the cloth as you clean to use a fresh section, and rinse it fairly frequently.

Stainless steel appliances are quite popular these days but they are very vulnerable to scratches from abrasive cleaners and require special cleaners—or at least they did until microfiber towels came along. You can clean and polish the stainless steel using the microfiber towel and plain water. Just remember to keep the towel rinsed clean so that it doesn't have grit in it. The side of the towel with the shorter nap will bring up the shine the best.

It isn't just stainless steel appliances that the towels can be used on. Stainless steel cooking pans that have gotten dull with use or detergent residues will shine right up with the microfiber towel. No polish needed. If you stainless steel flatware has dulled for the same reason, the towel will also work well.

Other shiny surfaces (like chrome toasters, coffee makers, etc.) can also be cleaned and buffed to a high shine. For the mirror finish on the chrome pieces, a final wipe with a paper towel eliminated some scattered droplets of water left by the towel. The silver-plated items brightened up if they had only a little tarnish beginning to show. The heavily tarnished items looked better for being rubbed with the microfiber towel, but I wouldn't suggest trying to really polish a very tarnished piece with the microfiber alone. Use a good silver polish first to remove heavy tarnish and then the microfiber towel to clean and shine the piece.

Small appliances with lots of little, raised buttons, such as food processors, juicers and blenders are a problem with the tiny gaps between the buttons collecting dust and food splatters. I folded the towel to fit into the spaces between the buttons and it cleaned the spaces.

But it isn't just the outside of the appliances that the microfiber towel can be used for. If you have a shiny interior plastic in the refrigerator, dishwasher or other appliance, the microfiber towel will get it clean. Dried on food will take some scrubbing with the towel, so keep turning the towel to a fresh area for it to work quickly.

The microwave—usually a pain in the neck—was really pretty easy to clean, inside and out with just the microfiber towel. It was a good test since it has enamel, steel, glass and plastic surfaces and food splatters on the inside. Previously, I'd used different cleaners for the inside and outside surfaces and removed the interior glass tray completely to wash separately in the sink. The microwave was cleaner on every surface using only water and the microfiber towel—and in a lot less time.

The only thing that the microfiber towels didn't get up were the really burnt on deposits on the stove top, oven racks and bottom. Those still needed to be softened and scraped, but the other (enameled) surfaces can be kept clean with regular wiping so the grease doesn't get a chance to build up to a shellac. If you have a rough or textured surface inside the oven, the towels won't do as good a job.

Cleaning Cupboards and Drawers

The outer surfaces of cupboards—whether glass, wood, laminate or plastic—are handled just like furniture. The damp microfiber towel does an excellent job with those. But where the microfiber towel really saved time was in cleaning the insides of cupboards and drawers. Anything that needed dusted, I wiped with the cloth as I took it out, then I rinsed out the cloth and wiped all of the inside surfaces. There was very little moisture left behind, so there wasn't much time needed for the cupboard to dry and I just put the items back in. One of the best features of microfiber towels is that *I know* the cupboards holding the food supplies, the dishes we eat and drink from, and the pans we cook with weren't exposed to cleaning chemical residues.

Countertops

Laminate and composition countertops clean very well with the microfiber towels, but if there is a stain in the surface itself, the towel won't get that out. Granite countertops that are easily scratched can be cleaned safely with the towel as long as the towel is rinsed clean. Sealed and finished wood counters are also effectively cleaned, but if you have an unfinished butcher block surface, the towel will only get off the surface residue. You will still need to use some sort of disinfecting agent on the wood to prevent cross-contamination of foods.

Tiled countertops and back splashes can be cleaned with the microfiber towel, and the tiles themselves are beautifully shined. But the grout between the tiles is a porous surface and isn't as cooperative. You'll still need to use a grout cleaning or bleaching product if the grout is really dirty.

Sinks

The surface of enameled, porcelain and stainless steel sinks will clean up nicely with a damp microfiber towel, but for stained areas, a penetrating bleaching agent is still needed. A gel product containing chlorine bleach can be used with the microfiber towel (such as *Chlorox Clean-Up* gel) but don't use the gritty cleaners since they can clog up the towel. To use the gel, apply it to the stained area directly from the bottle and let it sit for a short time following the directions on the product itself. Then using a wetted microfiber towel wipe down the sink. Rinse out the towel and wipe the sink a second time with the towel wrung out so that it is just damp.

If you have a specialty-product sink, check with the manufacturer for appropriate cleaning products so that you don't damage the surface. There are some unusual sinks on the market these days including those made of various types of stone, so be a little cautious if you have one of those.

Wastebaskets

Even if you use plastic wastebasket liners, wastebaskets get dirty from drips, leaks and the occasional miscalculated toss. Both the inner and outer surfaces of the plastic wastebaskets cleaned beautifully with a damp microfiber towel. Metal wastebaskets that have rusted at the bottom won't clean up well where the rust has pitted the surface, but everywhere else came clean.

Kitchen Cleaning in General

Microfiber towels do such a good job at picking up all of the various food particles, oils, and germs, that I noticed the damp towel went "sour" within a couple of hours of tackling the kitchen cleaning. If you aren't going to be running a load of wash fairly soon after using the towel, run a basin of water and pour in a teaspoon of chlorine bleach and let the towel soak. You can also freshen a damp towel by adding ¼ cup of household vinegar or lemon juice to the water. Let the towel sit in the water at least five minutes and then rinse it out again in plain water. I know that sounds like a bit of a nuisance, but when I considered how much more quickly I was able to get the kitchen clean and how many cleaning chemicals I didn't have to use, I thought it was a small price to pay.

Cast Iron and Seasoned Bakeware

These were two items that I found that *should not* be cleaned with a microfiber towel: cast iron pans and seasoned bakeware. Of course the towel would get their surfaces clean, but it works so well that it will also remove the seasoning that takes so long to establish.

Cleaning Fruits and Vegetables

If you're old enough to remember when cucumbers, apples and such were sold "as is," you're probably as thrilled as I am when I pick up one that has been heavily waxed. I was delighted to find out that a damp microfiber towel would remove the wax from the skins and leave a smooth surface. Be sure the towel is clean, use it damp, and just rub all over the fruit. Be sure to turn the cloth frequently because the wax will clog up the tiny fibers fairly quickly. After removing the wax rinse the fruit in plain water and rinse the towel in a basin of clean water.

CHAPTER 11

Bathroom Cleaning

I don't know anyone that actually likes to clean the bathroom, but microfiber towels have one feature that makes it worthwhile by itself. It picks up soap scum! The bathtub ring will respond to cleaning with a damp microfiber towel, but because the scum is so thick, keep turning the towel to have a fresh surface and rinse it frequently. Dried soap residue on shower walls and doors will also come off with a damp microfiber towel, but if it has accumulated for a long time, it may need extra elbow grease.

Using a microfiber towel, you can wipe down any smooth surface in the bathroom and it will leave a shine behind. The faucets and fixtures looked new.

We don't have hard water problems, but a friend tried the towels on her shower doors and they did a very good job. She had been cleaning the hard water stains with a chemical cleaner, and her recommendation was that for really heavy hard water deposits, the chemicals should probably be used as a first cleaning. Then, the microfiber towels work great for regular cleaning, and they seem to keep the deposits from coming back.

The various personal grooming items that accumulate in the bathroom are also easily and effectively cleaned with a damp microfiber towel. Hair dryers, curling irons, shavers and other small electrical appliances should be unplugged and cool to the touch before using the towels.

I was surprised at how well the microfiber towel worked to clean up hairbrushes. You have to rub the bristles well, but they looked much cleaner than with soap and water cleaning and felt smoother in use. The "gunk" that had built up on the bristles was gone and the brush felt like new.

For cleaning the toilet seats and any area where germs are a worry, you can use some disinfectant in rinsing the towel. But don't try to clean the toilet bowl itself. Microfiber towels won't clean the toilet bowl since it is full of water. Remember that being saturated with water deactivates the microfibers.

Bathroom cabinets and cupboards are cleaned just like any furniture or the cabinets in the kitchen. Because they are exposed to more moisture, the bathroom cabinets seem to collect a film more quickly than in other rooms. Using the microfiber towel for cleaning seemed to keep the cabinets looking good longer between cleanings.

Also, porcelain surfaces in the tub and sink shine like new since the towels remove any residues left from "wet" cleaning and any lingering soap scum. But rust stains from iron in the water won't be picked up since they are beneath the surface.

Mirrors in bathrooms collect a residue from condensation, too and the microfiber towels really make them shine. Use a paper towel for a follow-up drying if there are any water droplets left.

CHAPTER 12

Out and About

Since the microfiber towels are sold for "car detailing" I expected that they would do a good job, but I was surprised at how much dirt they picked up off of the interior surfaces of the car.

Cleaning the Car

The damp towels did a great job on the dashboard, and the various plastic and vinyl surfaces with just a quick wipe. On the gauges, I did follow up with a paper towel to make sure there weren't any streaks. The steering wheel—which seems to attract dirty fingerprints—looked almost new.

On the inside of the car, the thing I liked the most was being able to clean the windows without a commercial window cleaner. The inside window surfaces can develop a film from condensation during the cold months, which has previously required using a spray-on window cleaner and lots of paper towels. With just the damp microfiber towel, the windows came clean. I did do a finish drying with a paper towel. Remember to keep the towel well rinsed so that there isn't any grit in the towel to scratch the glass. (When doing the car, it is handy to have a bucket of clean water handy for frequent rinsing.)

One item that I think is important is to use the towels to clean the windshield wipers themselves. Ours had collected a lot of grit that was just going to be dragged across the windshield. I remember some of our old cars that had those circular scratches, from dirty windshield wipers.

The biggest surprise for me in the cars was the ability of the microfiber towel to clean off the "plush" upholstery. I just wiped it down with a damp towel and was surprised at how much dust, etc. showed up on the towel (and in the rinse water). If you have sticky spills on the upholstery, you'll probably need to wet them down with a little water first. I didn't have an example to test, but it's worth a try. Smooth upholstery of vinyl or leather is just like cleaning furniture (see Chapter 6).

If you have a very fancy car or special finish, I'll send you to the various web sites for auto detailers on the web. I wasn't concerned about taking our cars to a car show, just seeing if I could wash them on the outside without having to use any soaps or cleaners. I started on the windows first. They wiped clean very nicely and almost streak-free. Considering that we live in the woods and get tree sap spots fairly regularly, I was really impressed that they came right up. Because I was working on glass, and the cars were pretty dusty, I really kept the towels rinsed out.

Once the windows were done, I did the rest of the car as far as I could reach. From the paint, to the plastic headlight covers and the odd rubber seals, the towel did a great job. There was road oil on the paint in some places and it came right off, too. I did rinse out the towel frequently to keep the grit out of it, but otherwise, I didn't make any special effort. The cars looked very clean with less effort and best of all, I didn't need any chemicals, cleaners or detergents. I was impressed.

Recreational Vehicles and Campers

If you have an RV or camper, you will love how well microfiber towels can keep it clean. All of the smooth interior surfaces will wipe clean with just a damp towel, and using the towel conserves water. If you are on the road a lot, road dust and grime can collect quickly. The microfiber towels can keep that under control more easily (and more effectively) than regular dusting cloths or paper towels.

Sports Gear

Most sporting gear has the same types of surfaces as a car: metal, plastic, wood, vinyl, glass, etc., so I won't repeat that information. There is one other type of surface that I found on a backpack though: nylon with a heavy texture. The backpack was pretty dirty, and I didn't really expect the damp microfiber towel to make much improvement, but it did. I used the side of the cloth with the longer nap to get into the texture as much as possible and was amazed at how clean the fabric looked. That same sort of textured, woven nylon-ish sort of stuff is also on athletic shoes and various types of boots, so the microfiber towels should also work there.

One item of sports gear that I tested was a blue, foam exercise mat, which we also use outdoors. Usually microfiber towels don't get porous surfaces clean, so I was surprised to see that it did clean the exercise mat.

Yard and Garden

The outdoor furniture of metal, plastic and various fabrics cleaned up very well with just a damp microfiber towel. If you plan to do a lot of outdoor items, keep a bucket of water handy for rinsing the towel. Most of the types of items I worked with outdoors were so similar to the ones in the house or the car that I won't repeat that information. There were a couple of surprises, though. The picnic table made of painted wood had been exposed to strong sunlight and lots weather, so the paint had begun to chalk. The towel removed the chalking paint and the little bits of paint that had come loose from the surface.

I tested two watering cans, one of a heavy plastic and one with enamel paint over metal. Both cleaned up very well including the interiors, which had a lot of organic matter such as dried algae. The towel, however, was pretty ripe and took rinsing in water with some chlorine bleach before I wanted to use it for anything else.

The old flower pots I tested were of various types. The ceramic ones with a glazed surface cleaned up nicely. The unglazed pots didn't clean well in general, but the microfiber towel did remove some mineral salt rings that stood above the surface.

Camping

If you plan to go camping in an area where there isn't water available for washing dishes, microfiber towels can come in very handy. Wipe off the worst of the residue and then clean the surface of the dishes with a damp microfiber towel. Rinse the towel out and make sure that it gets a chance to dry out completely. Don't put the damp towel in a plastic bag or it will get really smelly.

Of course, a damp microfiber towel can also be used to keep camping gear clean too. Especially, if you going to put away the equipment for the season, wiping everything down with a damp microfiber towel will make sure that it is put away clean and ready for the next trip.

Travelling with a Microfiber Towel

Once you're used to how easy microfiber towels are to use, and how well they clean, you'll probably want to take them with you when you travel. They are a great way to make sure that motel surfaces are really clean. Whether it is the telephone, remote control, bathroom counter or headboard, a microfiber towel can make sure that the surface really is clean.

If you want to take a microfiber towel with you in luggage, don't pack it in a plastic bag. Instead use a breathe-able nylon (or other fabric) bag or zippered container. Some small make-up bags are perfect. When you arrive at your destination, soak and wring out the towel for use, leaving it on a counter. Use it as much as you need to, and then rinse it out again before you go to bed. Hang it to dry over a towel holder or the shower rail to dry overnight. Then it can be packed again.

Of course if you are travelling by car, you'll want the towel handy, so instead of packing it away. Rinse it and wring it out in the morning. Lay it across a seat back or wherever is handy as you drive.

CHAPTER 13

Kid Stuff

I have the distinct impression that microfiber towels could just be a busy parent's best friend. With all of the spills, dirty fingerprints, and who-knows-what that collects on toys, surfaces, equipment and such, it is a tremendous time-savings to be able to grab one damp towel and clean it all up. Well, almost all. If they use wax crayons on the wall, the microfiber towel will get it off, but permanent markers penetrate the surface so the towel can't reach it.

Then, of course, there is the concern about chemicals and children. By using a microfiber towel, you can do away with most of the chemicals and use a whole lot less of the rest. You'll still need the disinfectants, but with the ability of a microfiber towel to pick up bacteria, you can use the anti-bacterial soap only when it's really necessary.

If you have children (or anyone in the family) with hay fever or allergies to pollen, dusting with a microfiber cloth will pick it up off of surfaces. The microfibers will even pick up pet dander.

Baby Gear

Microfiber towels can clean all sorts of baby equipment including strollers, crib railings, walkers, toys, high chairs, diaper bags, etc. Smooth surfaces like plastic and metal will wipe clean with a damp towel, eliminating the need to use chemical cleaners. Keep a towel handy for quick clean-ups during the day and rinse it out well at night.

If you're going out with baby, a clean, damp microfiber towel can go along in the diaper bag, but don't put it in a plastic bag. Instead use a nylon or fabric bag that will let the towel breathe so it doesn't get sour. At restaurants, use the towel to wipe surfaces that baby may contact like high chairs and public changing tables. When you get home, just rinse and hang the towel to dry.

Little Kids

There are so many toys these days that have plastic buttons and knobs that are a problem to keep un-sticky with little kids. With a damp microfiber cloth, a quick wipe will get the surfaces clean. The towels will also work on game pieces, playing cards and small toys and dolls. They will pick up surface dirt from stuffed animals and similar plush toys.

If you have little ones in day care, talk to your day care provider about using microfiber towels too. There isn't any way to keep all of the surfaces clean, but using a microfiber towel regularly can help the spread of germs that is such a problem at day care facilities.

Bigger Kids

Microfiber towels are easy enough to use, (and because they work without chemicals) bigger kids can use them by themselves to keep their own prized possessions looking nice. No one in their right mind would trust a five-year-old with a bottle of spray cleaner, with all of the toxic warning on it. But children can use a damp microfiber towel safely. Just don't let them flush it down the toilet.

Especially since microfiber towels will be a novelty to the kids, they may get interested in helping with the housecleaning—and wouldn't that be nice?

CHAPTER 14

It Does Windows

Just a couple of weeks ago, the local newspaper ran an article about how to clean windows. Various chemicals, cleaners, cloths, squeegees and techniques of washing, rinsing and drying were discussed by several experts—but no mention at all of microfiber towels. They bemoaned the difficulty of oily residues and the coating that winter grime leaves on the outside. Different "professionals" waxed eloquent about how hard it was not to end up with streaks. After I'd cleaned my first window with a damp microfiber cloth, I couldn't help but feel sorry for those folks. Cleaning the windows was simple, done with plain water followed by a quick wipe with a paper towel to pick up the few water drops that were left behind. The inside and the outside surfaces came out squeaky clean, with no streaks!

The only caution to keep in mind is that the towel can pick up grit from the surface and if you rub hard, the grit—not the towel—can scratch the glass. So keep the towel rinsed out regularly. If you're doing the windowsill at the same time as the outside of the window, do it after you clean the glass and rinse the towel out before you do the next window.

There is a special microfiber towel that the auto detailers use just for glass. It is thinner than a general cleaning towel, with a shorter nap. The thinner towel can be wrung out more thoroughly so, in theory, it won't leave any water droplets behind. If you have to do lots of windows, all of the time, it is probably worthwhile to invest in a special glass cleaning towel, but I'm not going to. The regular microfiber cleaning towel leaves behind so little water that the paper towel I used for a final wipe didn't even get wet.

As for oily and sticky films left on the windows, the microfiber towel picked those up too. The window on the outside of our back door was so bad you could barely see through it. I made a point to turn the towel regularly, and it came out squeaky clean in just one session. In previous years, it has taken at least two and sometimes three rounds with glass cleaner to get it looking presentable. The towel's performance was really impressive.

If you are cleaning a really dirty window, be sure to keep turning the towel so that a fresh area is used. If you see a streak, that means that you need to get to a fresh spot on the towel that can pick up more of the residue.

With traditional cleaning methods, window streaks are caused by not getting all of the cleaner off, or where the cleaner itself isn't strong enough to dissolve the residues on the window. That's why the professionals are so concerned about rinsing the windows and using a squeegee to get them completely dry. With the microfiber towels, only water is used and the residue is physically removed from the surface, leaving it completely clean. A quick wipe with a paper towel is the only drying necessary.

Because of the oily component in the stuff that collects on window surfaces you'll want to add a drop of dish washing liquid or degreaser to the bucket or basin where you rinse out the towel, before you pour it down the drain. If you live in the city, the "grime" that collects on windows can have a lot of oil in it so you may need to add a little more soap or degreaser to the rinse water.

CHAPTER 15

Odds and Ends

The more enthused I became about using microfiber towels for cleaning, the more things I tried—and I freely admit that some of them were pretty strange. Once microfiber towels are in general cleaning use, there will probably be many "complete guides" published, but I'm including some of my experiments here just to encourage you to try things out yourself. Keep in mind the general principles for using microfiber towels in Chapter 5, and I'll bet you will discover even more applications for cleaning.

Adhesive Residues

That sticky residue that is left by price stickers or tape is a real pain to clean. I'd had some hanging around for months on a counter in the office where I'd left a piece of sealing tape too long. The microfiber towel picked it right up.

A damp towel also cleaned the residue from a window sticker. We don't have any bumper stickers I could test, but would suggest trying out the towels if you have persistent adhesive residues from those also.

Be cautious with price-sticker residue on paper surfaces though. I tried removing that from a coated paper box and the microfiber towel picked it up all right. Unfortunately the adhesive was so attached to the paper surface of the box, it took up the coating too.

Smoke Residues

The fine particles that make up smoke of any kind can form a hard coating on almost any surface—especially in the presence of moisture. That coating is really difficult to remove with conventional cleaning. As a test, I took a framed print that had been subject to smoke damage from a house fire to see if the microfiber towel would remove the coating. Someone had already tried to clean it conventionally, but took the finish off the picture frame in places. The microfiber towel cleaned the smoke coat from the glass quickly. On the painted frame, it took several rounds, but in the end the smoke coating had been removed without damage to the paint.

Smoke damage from a house fire is the most extreme, but living where we do we are regularly exposed to heavy smoke from forest fires, burning fields and pastures, burning of logging slash, etc. You can get smoke coatings from any source of smoke—a burned dinner on the stove, candles, fireplaces, tobacco, incense, etc. The microfiber towels make cleaning those residues and even hardened-on coatings much easier.

Dusting the Feather Duster

In my never-ending pursuit of the heavy dust here, I've tried various gadgets and dusters including feather dusters and those electostatic dusters on a pole that look like pom-poms. They would work fine for a while, but eventually our dust would win. The dusters just got clogged up and wouldn't pick up any more dust. I'd tried shaking them, vacuuming them and cleaning them with a damp rag but they just never worked well again.

Eventually, the electrostatic disposable dusting cloths came out and they seemed great, since when they got clogged up, I could just toss them out. I used a lot of those towels!

One early experiment I did with the microfiber towels was to try them on one of the disposable dustcloths, and was surprised that the towel actually picked up dust from the disposables. Eventually, I decided to try a damp towel on the feather duster and the electrostatic duster. The towel got off loads of dust and, with a little work to get to each feather, the dusters looked nearly new. And, the dusters started working like they were new again too.

No, the dusters aren't as efficient at cleaning as a microfiber towel, but once something has been cleaned with the towel, any dust that collects is just on the surface so the older dusters can do the job they were designed for.

Pet Grooming

Since it is spring as I write this, our dogs are shedding. When they get brushed, the shedding fur comes loose and so do old skin cells and the dust that was deep in their coats. Just to see what happened, I brushed one of the dogs and then used a damp microfiber towel for a rub down. The dog's coat was glistening clean and free of the debris raised by brushing. She knew she looked fabulous, too. The rinse water was pretty disgusting, so I added a drop of dish washing liquid to it before it went down the drain.

Pet Dishes

We have dogs and they have dishes. Their food dishes get washed regularly, but the water dishes seem to get just rinsed and refilled. On the surface of the water dishes a film of slobber seems to collect and it took serious scrubbing to remove with a paper towel. The microfiber towel cleaned off the film with just one pass.

Cleaning a Moth

As I was cleaning in the living room with a microfiber towel, an unlucky moth flapped in. I caught it but it left its dusty residue on my hand. Well, I couldn't resist. Not only did the microfiber towel pick up the dust from my hand, it completely cleaned off the wings of the late moth, leaving just the delicate, transparent structure. I can't think of any practical application for this bit of information, but if you have a moth or butterfly collection, I don't think you'll want to clean it with a microfiber towel.

Cleaning a Hooked Rug

The next thing I tried was a very old hooked rug, which had been handmade with narrow wool strips on a burlap base. Most often, experts advise that hooked rugs can be hand washed in cool water and mild soap, but some of the very old rugs are fragile and can be damaged, even by hand washing. I rubbed the surface gently with the microfiber towel and it was noticeably cleaner. The damp towel picked up quite a lot of dust from the surface that showed up in the rinse water.

Cleaning Scummy Stuff

Besides the soap scum that can collect around a bathtub or sink, there are other thick (and usually slimy) things that can be cleaned with a microfiber towel. Algae in fish tanks, mold or mildew that has had a chance to grow before it was discovered, etc. I found that the thick deposits clogged up the microfibers fairly quickly—though it did pick them up. I think it is a little more efficient to use a paper towel to get off the thickest deposits first, and then use the microfiber towel to really get the surface clean.

If you are tackling mold or mildew, remember that the microfiber towel will clean the surface but it won't kill the mold or mildew that has grown beneath the surface. For that you need a product with chlorine bleach in it.

Cleaning Textiles

Microfiber towels won't replace doing laundry in the conventional way, but they can be used for dusting off and removing surface lint and dirt from textiles that can't be washed or when washing isn't convenient. For example, I used a barely damp microfiber towel to remove the surface dust from cones and spools of thread. The towels also worked for removing the dust lines from jackets that had been hanging in the closet too long and to clean the cloth surfaces of chairpads that had gotten dusty.

The damp towels also picked up the surface lint from suits and pants. Surprisingly, it also removed the lint from a black sweater even though it had an uneven surface.

With soft-surface textiles, a gentle wipe (not hard rubbing) with the microfiber towel picked up the lint and dust and did a superficial cleaning. Soft surface textiles include wool, cottons and other clothing-type fabrics. You can also gently wipe down most upholstery fabrics to remove surface dust and fine particles.

Textiles made using fibers that have a hard surface (like nylon backpacks and windbreakers, goretex outerwear, etc.) could be rubbed with the towel and looked well-cleaned on the surface.

Very fragile textiles can be cleaned using a clean, dry microfiber towel that has been just misted with water. Use the towel to blot the surface—don't rub! The towel will pick up surface dust and other fine particles. The towel worked quite well to surface-clean the lacy dress of an antique doll. Very old textiles are fragile so a light, gentle touch is needed, and you should perfect your technique on a similar fabric before you try cleaning anything particularly precious.

Dusting Houseplants

Houseplants, like any surface around the house can collect dust and grime. Of course, microfiber towels can remove that, but be careful. Plant leaves have a natural coating of wax that helps to prevent the leaves from drying out. If you scrub too hard with a microfiber towel, you can remove that protective wax layer and end up doing more harm than good. To clean the leaves of houseplants that are only lightly dusty, a dry microfiber works best since it will attract the surface dust without removing the wax. For leaves that are really grimy, use a damp microfiber towel, but don't rub. Just stroke lightly.

Applying Waxes and Polishes

Microfiber towels do a marvelous job of polishing a surface, but for use around the house, it is not necessary to use the towels to apply polishes. Too much will attach to the towel itself, wasting the wax or polish. Instead, use a cotton rag or soft cloth to apply the polish or wax, as you would normally. When the surface is dry, polish the surface with a damp microfiber towel to bring up a really nice shine.

Construction Dust

We are regularly involved in a construction or remodelling project around the place. The fine dust from fiberglass insulation and drywall sanding has always presented a big problem. The micofiber towels picked it right up and it rinsed down the drain, which is a tremendous improvement as far as I am concerned.

Outdoor Painting Preparation

If you have outdoor painted furniture or painted siding, the old paint can begin to chalk off after it has been exposed to strong sunlight and weather extremes. A damp microfiber towel will remove the chalking and small pieces of paint that have come loose from the surface.

Cleaning You

You may be wondering if microfibers can be used to clean people too. There are special towels that are being made for just that purpose, since they can clean skin and remove oils, dirt, etc. The specialty towels have different weaves, fiber contents and textures than the regular cleaning towels, but once you understand the principles of how microfibers work, you'll be able to use those towels more effectively.

CHAPTER 16

Domestic Science

Before World War Two, schools taught classes in "Domestic Science"—what we now call "Home Economics." When it comes to learning about what microfiber towels can do, I think the older term is probably more appropriate.

Micofiber towels are so new to most of us that we really have a hard time believing what they can do. I know I did. In this chapter are several experiments that you can try to see for yourself how well microfiber cleans.

Half-and-half

An easy way to demonstrate their abilities is to clean half of a surface the way you always have, and the other half with a microfiber towel. You can try this on any hard surface, but windows make a really good test. Clean half of the window however you usually would. Clean the other half with a damp microfiber towel and a quick wipe with a paper towel to pick up any loose water droplets. (See the chapter on cleaning windows for more hints.) You may not think there is a whole lot of difference at first, but wait a few days and go back and look at the window. The part cleaned with the microfiber towel won't collect dust as fast as the other half.

Comparison Cleaning

For this experiment you don't need any special equipment. Find one area that you want to use as a test and clean it as you normally would. Then go back in about an hour (just to make sure that the surface is dry) and clean the same area with a damp microfiber towel. Just do that one area. Then run cool or lukewarm water in the sink and rinse the towel by dunking it in the water. All of the stuff that shows up in the rinse water was left behind by the regular cleaning method, but picked up by the microfiber towel. I tried this on a coffee table (cleaned with a spray wax and paper towel), the floor in the home office (swept and mopped) and the top of the stove (cleaned with a surface cleaner). In all three cases, the microfiber towel picked up quite a lot that my regular cleaning had left behind.

What's on My Upholstery?

You can do this experiment in the sink, but it is really more graphic if you have a glass mixing bowl and a magnifying glass. Fill the mixing bowl with clean tap water (cool to lukewarm). Vacuum your upholstery as you normally would, or, if your upholstery looks clean, you can skip that step. Using a damp microfiber towel, rub down any leather or vinyl upholstery and wipe the surfaces of cloth upholstery. Turn the towel often so that it works most effectively. Then rinse the towel in the water in the mixing bowl. Dip it in and out of the water several times and then wring it out (also into the mixing bowl).

Use the magnifying glass to look at the rinse water. Notice anything moving? Those are the dust mites, which are so small that even with a magnifying glass, you can't really see them, just that they are moving. Let the water sit for a few hours (or overnight). You'll notice that some of the dust particles have settled to the bottom of the bowl, but most of the water still looks dirty. The particles that haven't settled out are the extremely small ones of dust, dander, pollen, etc. There will probably also be a fine layer of wax that has collected at the surface. That can be residue from furniture cleaners but also probably contains body oils. (When you're done, you will of course want to wash the mixing bowl out really well!)

I have a household microscope (oh, don't groan) and took a sample of the water from the mixing bowl. With the microscope, the dust mites and the bacteria in the water could be plainly seen. It was, I admit, not pretty.

The same experiment can be done on any surface, of course, floors, keyboards, telephones, walls and so on. A great feature of this experiment is that the kids can participate and you just might get them interested in doing a little more cleaning up. Grade school science teachers can also use it to demonstrate several basic principles.

CHAPTER 17

Real Help for the Discouraged Homemaker

People may think that because I've written about cleaning house that I am one of those perfectionist housekeepers whose homes always gleam. Nothing could be further from the truth. For years, I've been in the same mess (literally) as lots of women who are busy with family, work and a whole list of obligations. House cleaning was way down on the priority list, and a lot of it just got "let go." After a period of ill-health (and especially with our heavy dust) things got to looking so bad that I wouldn't invite anyone over. I'm not exaggerating.

I so-clearly remember an unexpected visit from my dear friend Peggy. Thoroughly embarrassed at the state of the house, I offered coffee at the picnic table instead. Unfortunately, the time came when Peggy needed to come in, and I could only apologize and explain that the house was a disaster area. Bless her heart, Peggy's only comment was "Don't worry. I know how it is and I've seen worse."

So, you can understand that I really was in good standing with the league of "discouraged homemakers"—possibly even in the running for poster child. When a person cleans something, and an hour later it needs dusting again, it becomes pointless to even try to keep up. Of course, the cleaning problems didn't go away, and occasionally I would just take a day and try a deep cleaning on the worst places. But even deep cleaning didn't last very long.

I noticed that when I began to learn how to really use the microfiber towels, my attitude about house cleaning improved. Not only did everything look cleaner than it had; I spent a lot less effort and time getting it that way. It was a *delightful* bonus to find that things even stayed cleaner longer. I enjoy a clean house as much as anyone, so the results really lifted my spirits.

No, our dust problem hasn't gone away. Dust is just a part of living in the country, but it isn't nearly as big a problem as it once was. The microfiber towels leave surfaces so clean that they just don't *attract* the dust like they used to. Where I had to dust every day, I can now dust once a week. That alone is a miracle.

It is my hope that getting the word out about how to use these towels that other discouraged homemakers will find that there is some real help for their dilemma.

APPENDIX

What are Microfiber Towels and How Do They Work Their Magic

First, let me say that the following chapter is very simplified, but I feel strongly that people need to know *why* microfiber cleaning towels work to be able to use effectively. Please note also that information about the workings of microfiber towels was not available from any source that I could find (otherwise I would certainly acknowledge it). Instead, this information is a product of my own frustration in trying to teach myself how to use a microfiber towel.

There were several features that I observed, and in dusting off my college chemistry and physics, I finally came to a working theory that explained the unique phenomena that I had observed. It was only when I could explain to my own satisfaction, and reliably test the result that I felt confident in writing this information.

The key questions that I felt had to be answered were:

1. How can a microfiber towel pick up oil and grease using only water?

2. Why do the towels rinse clean, also using only water?

3. Why do the towels work better without solvents than with them?

I believe I have identified the mechanisms at work, but I also know that there is a lot more to those mechanisms than I can relate here. What I can say is that it was an interesting exercise and would be a good lab project for students.

Microfibers Aren't New

Microfibers were developed by the E. I. Du Pont de Nemours & Company, Inc., and they first produced them commercially in 1989. Olsson Cleaning Technology in Sweden discovered that splitting microfibers greatly improved their cleaning ability. One of the first industries to use microfiber towels were companies that maintained "clean rooms" for working on computer chips, since the tiniest dust particles could interfere with the process. In the last few years, microfiber towels were discovered by the people who clean automobiles for shows or for car dealers. These auto detailers have any number of different types of surfaces that they need to keep perfectly cleaned and shined, and a microfiber towel will clean them all.

On several internet sites was the historical information about the development of microfibers and even micro-photographs of the fibers themselves. Those photographs were extremely helpful in deriving the mechanisms that make the towels work.

Damp Microfiber Towels—the Real Magic

In my early days of using microfiber towels for house cleaning, I kept trying to "help" the towels on the more-is-better idea. If a little dampness in the towel works well, more should be better. If the towel can clean so well just using water, it should clean better using soap and water. Every time I tried to "help" the towel it worked less effectively or not any better than a paper towel or cotton rag. Only when I quit "helping" did the towel demonstrate its outstanding cleaning ability.

The microfiber towel clearly did its best cleaning when it was only a little damp and finally it dawned on me that the key to its functioning must be a property of water itself. Water is a unique molecule and it has been the basis of cleaning for thousands of years because of its ability to dissolve so many other things. For that reason, it is known as the "universal solvent" but of course water can't dissolve oil, so the microfiber towels had to be operating using some other characteristic of water.

When I began to think at the microscopic scale of microfibers, it finally dawned on me that water spread that thinly over such a large surface area had to have a dramatic amount of surface tension. The absorbent fiber in the core of the microfiber would attract the water molecules to the center of the fiber with a wicking action. The water molecules in the very tiny grooves of the microfiber would want to hold together, due to surface tension, so any tiny dust particle would be held in the groove. When the towel was submerged in water, the surface tension would be broken and the dust particles would be released into the water.

Once I began considering surface tension as the operating mechanism, I could also explain why soaps, detergents and surfactants wouldn't "help" a microfiber towel. Those agents destroy the surface tension of water. What I came to realize is that for all of human history we have be using the chemical properties of water. With the development of microfibers, we can now use the physics of water to clean in a more effective way.

SOURCES OF SUPPLY

Microfiber towels are available at auto supply stores, tire stores, car dealers and almost every shop that relates to vehicles. Just be sure to note the specifications for a good cleaning towel in Chapter 4. There are also many outlets on the internet selling various grades and types of towels. When purchasing towels over the internet, be sure that the dealer is carrying "split"microfiber towels. Below are a few of the sources I found.

Grakar Specialty Products
www.grakar.com

Impressive Reflections
www.heavymetalpolish.com

Autotopia Car Care
www.autotopia-carcare.com

As of this writing (May 2005), there aren't any websites with information about house cleaning with microfiber towels. I expect that will change very rapidly so a search for "Super-Green Clean" or "Microfiber House Cleaning" should bring results before too long.

Additional copies of this book are available on the internet at Amazon.com and Barnes & Noble (www.bn.com).

ABOUT THE AUTHOR

Appaloosa Moose is the *nom de plume* of D. B. Gray, a former wildlife biologist and regional environmental planner specializing in water quality. She is now a fiber artist and lives with her husband in their hand-built home in the mountains of Idaho. About the time that Mrs. Gray began exploring cleaning with microfiber towels a young moose appeared and took up residence in the neighborhood. Ms. Appaloosa Moose, as she came to be called, has graciously consented to the use of her name on the cover. Well, she hasn't complained anyway.

JOIN THE
Super-Green Clean
REVOLUTION

Once you've experienced the cleaning abilities of microfiber towels, you'll want to share the experience. The towels make wonderful gifts, and friends and family will appreciate the time-savings and chemical-free cleaning. But, because microfiber towels work so differently than cotton or paper towels, giving someone a microfiber towel without giving them instructions on how to use it won't be any help.

I believe strongly in the ability of microfiber towels to make our lives better by saving time, cleaning better, and eliminating the need for many household chemicals. Because I do, I am including several tear-out pages at the end of this book. Feel free to cut out a page to give to a friend when you give her a towel. That way she will know the basics of how to use it and care for it.

The word about using microfiber towels will spread from person to person as we all share our experiences in using this new technology. This book is just the beginning, I'm sure. I'm also sure that the towels can make a very positive changes in many ways and that in a few years, they will be so natural a part of our cleaning routines that we'll wonder how we ever got along without them.

P. S. When you have used microfiber towels for a few months, you'll probably notice all of the chemical cleaners in your cupboard that you haven't been using. Please don't pour them down the drain. They will end up in the water supply. Instead, take them to a hazardous waste collection facility for safe disposal.

How to use a microfiber towel for cleaning house…

Extracted with the permission of the author from:
The Super-Green Clean: Using Microfiber Towels to Clean Nearly Anything with Plain Water, by Appaloosa Moose

A microfiber towel will pick up dust, surface residues, microscopic particles and even grease and oil with plain tap water; but for a towel to work its magic, it must be handled the right way.

With a brand new towel, fill a sink or basin with cool to lukewarm tap water. Hold the towel underwater for several seconds until it becomes saturated. Then wring it out. Repeat the process.

To wring out a towel, fold the towel in quarters, then roll it up and wring out as much moisture as you can. Microfiber towels clean most effectively when they are just dampened, not wet.

To clean with a microfiber towel, wipe any smooth surface with the towel open (not wadded up). Keep turning the towel as you clean to use a fresh area, for the most efficient cleaning. If the towel is leaving streaks of moisture behind, it is too wet, and should be wrung out again. If the towel is leaving streaks of dirt or grime, move to a fresh area of the towel or rinse the towel.

Do not use soaps, detergents, cleaners or degreasers with a microfiber towel. The chemicals will prevent the towel from working.

When the towel gets dirty, fill a sink or container with cool to lukewarm water. Swish the towel around in the water. Then, holding the edge of the towel, dunk it in and out of the water several times. When the towel stops leaving more dirt in the water, it is ready to reuse. Wring it out and use it for cleaning again.

When you are finished cleaning, rinse and wring the towel once more. Hang it to dry overnight and it can be re-used day after day. When it gets really dirty and won't rinse clean, the towel can be machine-washed following the directions on the next page.

NOTE: Microfiber towels by themselves won't scratch glass or delicate surfaces. But they are very good at picking up grit (particles of dirt or sand). If you have grit in the towel and wash a window, you stand the chance of scratching it. So if you're going to clean windows, glass objects or other delicate surfaces, make sure to use a freshly clean, well-rinsed towel.

Never let wet paint, glazes, glues or milk dry on the surface of a microfiber towel. They can attach permanently to the fibers. If you can't rinse out the towel right away, drop it in a basin of water to soak in the meantime.

Basic Directions for Machine Washing:

- **NEVER** use hot water with a microfiber towel; the fibers will shrink and not work as well (the tiny channels close up). This means cool to lukewarm water to rinse the towel with as you're working, and the "cool" or "cold" setting on the washing machine.
- **NEVER** expose the microfiber towel to heat. Use the coolest ("delicate") setting on the dryer, don't iron it (why would anyone?) and don't use it on hot objects. With high temperatures the synthetic fibers will melt.
- **NEVER** use a fabric softener with a microfiber towel. Not in the washer and not in the dryer. The chemicals in the softeners will coat the microfibers, keeping them from working like they should.
- **NEVER** wash a microfiber towel with regular terry cloth towels, socks or other items that shed a lot of lint. The microfiber towel will pick up the lint from cotton towels and get clogged up. Instead, wash the microfiber towels in a load with other fabrics that also need cool water. What I have learned is that the towels actually wash up the best if you do a load of just the microfiber towels, using about ¼ as much laundry detergent as for a regular load. The towels need lots of water, though so only put about half as many in the wash as you would with regular fabrics. I tested a load just going through the rinse cycle with four towels, and they were just about as clean as the ones that had gone through the wash cycle too.
- **AVOID** powdered laundry products since some of them don't dissolve all of the way and detergent grains can get picked up by the microfibers. The same is true if you want to use a disinfectant with the towel—stick to the liquids. You can add bleach to the wash load, but only use about half as much as you would for bleaching whites. (The exact amount will depend on how large your washing machine is.)

By learning to use microfiber towels, you can avoid using many household cleaning chemicals and contribute to cleaner air and water as well as having a super-green clean home. Microfiber towels leave surfaces cleaner than conventional methods so things stay cleaner longer, too. To learn more about how these towels work, see *The Super-Green Clean: Using Microfiber Towels to Clean Nearly Anything with Plain Water,* by Applaloosa Moose. The book is available online at Amazon.com and Barnes & Noble.

How to use a microfiber towel for cleaning house…

Extracted with the permission of the author from:
The Super-Green Clean: Using Microfiber Towels to Clean Nearly Anything with Plain Water, by Appaloosa Moose

A microfiber towel will pick up dust, surface residues, microscopic particles and even grease and oil with plain tap water; but for a towel to work its magic, it must be handled the right way.

With a brand new towel, fill a sink or basin with cool to lukewarm tap water. Hold the towel underwater for several seconds until it becomes saturated. Then wring it out. Repeat the process.

To wring out a towel, fold the towel in quarters, then roll it up and wring out as much moisture as you can. Microfiber towels clean most effectively when they are just dampened, not wet.

To clean with a microfiber towel, wipe any smooth surface with the towel open (not wadded up). Keep turning the towel as you clean to use a fresh area, for the most efficient cleaning. If the towel is leaving streaks of moisture behind, it is too wet, and should be wrung out again. If the towel is leaving streaks of dirt or grime, move to a fresh area of the towel or rinse the towel.

Do not use soaps, detergents, cleaners or degreasers with a microfiber towel. The chemicals will prevent the towel from working.

When the towel gets dirty, fill a sink or container with cool to lukewarm water. Swish the towel around in the water. Then, holding the edge of the towel, dunk it in and out of the water several times. When the towel stops leaving more dirt in the water, it is ready to reuse. Wring it out and use it for cleaning again.

When you are finished cleaning, rinse and wring the towel once more. Hang it to dry overnight and it can be re-used day after day. When it gets really dirty and won't rinse clean, the towel can be machine-washed following the directions on the next page.

NOTE: Microfiber towels by themselves won't scratch glass or delicate surfaces. But they are very good at picking up grit (particles of dirt or sand). If you have grit in the towel and wash a window, you stand the chance of scratching it. So if you're going to clean windows, glass objects or other delicate surfaces, make sure to use a freshly clean, well-rinsed towel.

Never let wet paint, glazes, glues or milk dry on the surface of a microfiber towel. They can attach permanently to the fibers. If you can't rinse out the towel right away, drop it in a basin of water to soak in the meantime.

Basic Directions for Machine Washing:

- **NEVER** use hot water with a microfiber towel; the fibers will shrink and not work as well (the tiny channels close up). This means cool to lukewarm water to rinse the towel with as you're working, and the "cool" or "cold" setting on the washing machine.
- **NEVER** expose the microfiber towel to heat. Use the coolest ("delicate") setting on the dryer, don't iron it (why would anyone?) and don't use it on hot objects. With high temperatures the synthetic fibers will melt.
- **NEVER** use a fabric softener with a microfiber towel. Not in the washer and not in the dryer. The chemicals in the softeners will coat the microfibers, keeping them from working like they should.
- **NEVER** wash a microfiber towel with regular terry cloth towels, socks or other items that shed a lot of lint. The microfiber towel will pick up the lint from cotton towels and get clogged up. Instead, wash the microfiber towels in a load with other fabrics that also need cool water. What I have learned is that the towels actually wash up the best if you do a load of just the microfiber towels, using about ¼ as much laundry detergent as for a regular load. The towels need lots of water, though so only put about half as many in the wash as you would with regular fabrics. I tested a load just going through the rinse cycle with four towels, and they were just about as clean as the ones that had gone through the wash cycle too.
- **AVOID** powdered laundry products since some of them don't dissolve all of the way and detergent grains can get picked up by the microfibers. The same is true if you want to use a disinfectant with the towel—stick to the liquids. You can add bleach to the wash load, but only use about half as much as you would for bleaching whites. (The exact amount will depend on how large your washing machine is.)

By learning to use microfiber towels, you can avoid using many household cleaning chemicals and contribute to cleaner air and water as well as having a super-green clean home. Microfiber towels leave surfaces cleaner than conventional methods so things stay cleaner longer, too. To learn more about how these towels work, see *The Super-Green Clean: Using Microfiber Towels to Clean Nearly Anything with Plain Water,* by Applaloosa Moose. The book is available online at Amazon.com and Barnes & Noble.

How to use a microfiber towel for cleaning house…

Extracted with the permission of the author from:
The Super-Green Clean: Using Microfiber Towels to Clean Nearly Anything with Plain Water, by Appaloosa Moose

A microfiber towel will pick up dust, surface residues, microscopic particles and even grease and oil with plain tap water; but for a towel to work its magic, it must be handled the right way.

With a brand new towel, fill a sink or basin with cool to lukewarm tap water. Hold the towel underwater for several seconds until it becomes saturated. Then wring it out. Repeat the process.

To wring out a towel, fold the towel in quarters, then roll it up and wring out as much moisture as you can. Microfiber towels clean most effectively when they are just dampened, not wet.

To clean with a microfiber towel, wipe any smooth surface with the towel open (not wadded up). Keep turning the towel as you clean to use a fresh area, for the most efficient cleaning. If the towel is leaving streaks of moisture behind, it is too wet, and should be wrung out again. If the towel is leaving streaks of dirt or grime, move to a fresh area of the towel or rinse the towel.

Do not use soaps, detergents, cleaners or degreasers with a microfiber towel. The chemicals will prevent the towel from working.

When the towel gets dirty, fill a sink or container with cool to lukewarm water. Swish the towel around in the water. Then, holding the edge of the towel, dunk it in and out of the water several times. When the towel stops leaving more dirt in the water, it is ready to reuse. Wring it out and use it for cleaning again.

When you are finished cleaning, rinse and wring the towel once more. Hang it to dry overnight and it can be re-used day after day. When it gets really dirty and won't rinse clean, the towel can be machine-washed following the directions on the next page.

NOTE: Microfiber towels by themselves won't scratch glass or delicate surfaces. But they are very good at picking up grit (particles of dirt or sand). If you have grit in the towel and wash a window, you stand the chance of scratching it. So if you're going to clean windows, glass objects or other delicate surfaces, make sure to use a freshly clean, well-rinsed towel.

Never let wet paint, glazes, glues or milk dry on the surface of a microfiber towel. They can attach permanently to the fibers. If you can't rinse out the towel right away, drop it in a basin of water to soak in the meantime.

Basic Directions for Machine Washing:

- **NEVER** use hot water with a microfiber towel; the fibers will shrink and not work as well (the tiny channels close up). This means cool to lukewarm water to rinse the towel with as you're working, and the "cool" or "cold" setting on the washing machine.
- **NEVER** expose the microfiber towel to heat. Use the coolest ("delicate") setting on the dryer, don't iron it (why would anyone?) and don't use it on hot objects. With high temperatures the synthetic fibers will melt.
- **NEVER** use a fabric softener with a microfiber towel. Not in the washer and not in the dryer. The chemicals in the softeners will coat the microfibers, keeping them from working like they should.
- **NEVER** wash a microfiber towel with regular terry cloth towels, socks or other items that shed a lot of lint. The microfiber towel will pick up the lint from cotton towels and get clogged up. Instead, wash the microfiber towels in a load with other fabrics that also need cool water. What I have learned is that the towels actually wash up the best if you do a load of just the microfiber towels, using about ¼ as much laundry detergent as for a regular load. The towels need lots of water, though so only put about half as many in the wash as you would with regular fabrics. I tested a load just going through the rinse cycle with four towels, and they were just about as clean as the ones that had gone through the wash cycle too.
- **AVOID** powdered laundry products since some of them don't dissolve all of the way and detergent grains can get picked up by the microfibers. The same is true if you want to use a disinfectant with the towel—stick to the liquids. You can add bleach to the wash load, but only use about half as much as you would for bleaching whites. (The exact amount will depend on how large your washing machine is.)

By learning to use microfiber towels, you can avoid using many household cleaning chemicals and contribute to cleaner air and water as well as having a super-green clean home. Microfiber towels leave surfaces cleaner than conventional methods so things stay cleaner longer, too. To learn more about how these towels work, see *The Super-Green Clean: Using Microfiber Towels to Clean Nearly Anything with Plain Water,* by Applaloosa Moose. The book is available online at Amazon.com and Barnes & Noble.

How to use a microfiber towel for cleaning house...

Extracted with the permission of the author from:
The Super-Green Clean: Using Microfiber Towels to Clean Nearly Anything with Plain Water, by Appaloosa Moose

A microfiber towel will pick up dust, surface residues, microscopic particles and even grease and oil with plain tap water; but for a towel to work its magic, it must be handled the right way.

With a brand new towel, fill a sink or basin with cool to lukewarm tap water. Hold the towel underwater for several seconds until it becomes saturated. Then wring it out. Repeat the process.

To wring out a towel, fold the towel in quarters, then roll it up and wring out as much moisture as you can. Microfiber towels clean most effectively when they are just dampened, not wet.

To clean with a microfiber towel, wipe any smooth surface with the towel open (not wadded up). Keep turning the towel as you clean to use a fresh area, for the most efficient cleaning. If the towel is leaving streaks of moisture behind, it is too wet, and should be wrung out again. If the towel is leaving streaks of dirt or grime, move to a fresh area of the towel or rinse the towel.

Do not use soaps, detergents, cleaners or degreasers with a microfiber towel. The chemicals will prevent the towel from working.

When the towel gets dirty, fill a sink or container with cool to lukewarm water. Swish the towel around in the water. Then, holding the edge of the towel, dunk it in and out of the water several times. When the towel stops leaving more dirt in the water, it is ready to reuse. Wring it out and use it for cleaning again.

When you are finished cleaning, rinse and wring the towel once more. Hang it to dry overnight and it can be re-used day after day. When it gets really dirty and won't rinse clean, the towel can be machine-washed following the directions on the next page.

NOTE: Microfiber towels by themselves won't scratch glass or delicate surfaces. But they are very good at picking up grit (particles of dirt or sand). If you have grit in the towel and wash a window, you stand the chance of scratching it. So if you're going to clean windows, glass objects or other delicate surfaces, make sure to use a freshly clean, well-rinsed towel.

Never let wet paint, glazes, glues or milk dry on the surface of a microfiber towel. They can attach permanently to the fibers. If you can't rinse out the towel right away, drop it in a basin of water to soak in the meantime.

Basic Directions for Machine Washing:

- **NEVER** use hot water with a microfiber towel; the fibers will shrink and not work as well (the tiny channels close up). This means cool to lukewarm water to rinse the towel with as you're working, and the "cool" or "cold" setting on the washing machine.
- **NEVER** expose the microfiber towel to heat. Use the coolest ("delicate") setting on the dryer, don't iron it (why would anyone?) and don't use it on hot objects. With high temperatures the synthetic fibers will melt.
- **NEVER** use a fabric softener with a microfiber towel. Not in the washer and not in the dryer. The chemicals in the softeners will coat the microfibers, keeping them from working like they should.
- **NEVER** wash a microfiber towel with regular terry cloth towels, socks or other items that shed a lot of lint. The microfiber towel will pick up the lint from cotton towels and get clogged up. Instead, wash the microfiber towels in a load with other fabrics that also need cool water. What I have learned is that the towels actually wash up the best if you do a load of just the microfiber towels, using about ¼ as much laundry detergent as for a regular load. The towels need lots of water, though so only put about half as many in the wash as you would with regular fabrics. I tested a load just going through the rinse cycle with four towels, and they were just about as clean as the ones that had gone through the wash cycle too.
- **AVOID** powdered laundry products since some of them don't dissolve all of the way and detergent grains can get picked up by the microfibers. The same is true if you want to use a disinfectant with the towel—stick to the liquids. You can add bleach to the wash load, but only use about half as much as you would for bleaching whites. (The exact amount will depend on how large your washing machine is.)

By learning to use microfiber towels, you can avoid using many household cleaning chemicals and contribute to cleaner air and water as well as having a super-green clean home. Microfiber towels leave surfaces cleaner than conventional methods so things stay cleaner longer, too. To learn more about how these towels work, see *The Super-Green Clean: Using Microfiber Towels to Clean Nearly Anything with Plain Water,* by Applaloosa Moose. The book is available online at Amazon.com and Barnes & Noble.

How to use a microfiber towel for cleaning house…

Extracted with the permission of the author from:
The Super-Green Clean: Using Microfiber Towels to Clean Nearly Anything with Plain Water, by Appaloosa Moose

A microfiber towel will pick up dust, surface residues, microscopic particles and even grease and oil with plain tap water; but for a towel to work its magic, it must be handled the right way.

With a brand new towel, fill a sink or basin with cool to lukewarm tap water. Hold the towel underwater for several seconds until it becomes saturated. Then wring it out. Repeat the process.

To wring out a towel, fold the towel in quarters, then roll it up and wring out as much moisture as you can. Microfiber towels clean most effectively when they are just dampened, not wet.

To clean with a microfiber towel, wipe any smooth surface with the towel open (not wadded up). Keep turning the towel as you clean to use a fresh area, for the most efficient cleaning. If the towel is leaving streaks of moisture behind, it is too wet, and should be wrung out again. If the towel is leaving streaks of dirt or grime, move to a fresh area of the towel or rinse the towel.

Do not use soaps, detergents, cleaners or degreasers with a microfiber towel. The chemicals will prevent the towel from working.

When the towel gets dirty, fill a sink or container with cool to lukewarm water. Swish the towel around in the water. Then, holding the edge of the towel, dunk it in and out of the water several times. When the towel stops leaving more dirt in the water, it is ready to reuse. Wring it out and use it for cleaning again.

When you are finished cleaning, rinse and wring the towel once more. Hang it to dry overnight and it can be re-used day after day. When it gets really dirty and won't rinse clean, the towel can be machine-washed following the directions on the next page.

NOTE: Microfiber towels by themselves won't scratch glass or delicate surfaces. But they are very good at picking up grit (particles of dirt or sand). If you have grit in the towel and wash a window, you stand the chance of scratching it. So if you're going to clean windows, glass objects or other delicate surfaces, make sure to use a freshly clean, well-rinsed towel.

Never let wet paint, glazes, glues or milk dry on the surface of a microfiber towel. They can attach permanently to the fibers. If you can't rinse out the towel right away, drop it in a basin of water to soak in the meantime.

Basic Directions for Machine Washing:

- **NEVER** use hot water with a microfiber towel; the fibers will shrink and not work as well (the tiny channels close up). This means cool to lukewarm water to rinse the towel with as you're working, and the "cool" or "cold" setting on the washing machine.
- **NEVER** expose the microfiber towel to heat. Use the coolest ("delicate") setting on the dryer, don't iron it (why would anyone?) and don't use it on hot objects. With high temperatures the synthetic fibers will melt.
- **NEVER** use a fabric softener with a microfiber towel. Not in the washer and not in the dryer. The chemicals in the softeners will coat the microfibers, keeping them from working like they should.
- **NEVER** wash a microfiber towel with regular terry cloth towels, socks or other items that shed a lot of lint. The microfiber towel will pick up the lint from cotton towels and get clogged up. Instead, wash the microfiber towels in a load with other fabrics that also need cool water. What I have learned is that the towels actually wash up the best if you do a load of just the microfiber towels, using about ¼ as much laundry detergent as for a regular load. The towels need lots of water, though so only put about half as many in the wash as you would with regular fabrics. I tested a load just going through the rinse cycle with four towels, and they were just about as clean as the ones that had gone through the wash cycle too.
- **AVOID** powdered laundry products since some of them don't dissolve all of the way and detergent grains can get picked up by the microfibers. The same is true if you want to use a disinfectant with the towel—stick to the liquids. You can add bleach to the wash load, but only use about half as much as you would for bleaching whites. (The exact amount will depend on how large your washing machine is.)

By learning to use microfiber towels, you can avoid using many household cleaning chemicals and contribute to cleaner air and water as well as having a super-green clean home. Microfiber towels leave surfaces cleaner than conventional methods so things stay cleaner longer, too. To learn more about how these towels work, see *The Super-Green Clean: Using Microfiber Towels to Clean Nearly Anything with Plain Water,* by Applaloosa Moose. The book is available online at Amazon.com and Barnes & Noble.

How to use a microfiber towel for cleaning house...

Extracted with the permission of the author from:
The Super-Green Clean: Using Microfiber Towels to Clean Nearly Anything with Plain Water, by Appaloosa Moose

A microfiber towel will pick up dust, surface residues, microscopic particles and even grease and oil with plain tap water; but for a towel to work its magic, it must be handled the right way.

With a brand new towel, fill a sink or basin with cool to lukewarm tap water. Hold the towel underwater for several seconds until it becomes saturated. Then wring it out. Repeat the process.

To wring out a towel, fold the towel in quarters, then roll it up and wring out as much moisture as you can. Microfiber towels clean most effectively when they are just dampened, not wet.

To clean with a microfiber towel, wipe any smooth surface with the towel open (not wadded up). Keep turning the towel as you clean to use a fresh area, for the most efficient cleaning. If the towel is leaving streaks of moisture behind, it is too wet, and should be wrung out again. If the towel is leaving streaks of dirt or grime, move to a fresh area of the towel or rinse the towel.

Do not use soaps, detergents, cleaners or degreasers with a microfiber towel. The chemicals will prevent the towel from working.

When the towel gets dirty, fill a sink or container with cool to lukewarm water. Swish the towel around in the water. Then, holding the edge of the towel, dunk it in and out of the water several times. When the towel stops leaving more dirt in the water, it is ready to reuse. Wring it out and use it for cleaning again.

When you are finished cleaning, rinse and wring the towel once more. Hang it to dry overnight and it can be re-used day after day. When it gets really dirty and won't rinse clean, the towel can be machine-washed following the directions on the next page.

NOTE: Microfiber towels by themselves won't scratch glass or delicate surfaces. But they are very good at picking up grit (particles of dirt or sand). If you have grit in the towel and wash a window, you stand the chance of scratching it. So if you're going to clean windows, glass objects or other delicate surfaces, make sure to use a freshly clean, well-rinsed towel.

Never let wet paint, glazes, glues or milk dry on the surface of a microfiber towel. They can attach permanently to the fibers. If you can't rinse out the towel right away, drop it in a basin of water to soak in the meantime.

Basic Directions for Machine Washing:

- **NEVER** use hot water with a microfiber towel; the fibers will shrink and not work as well (the tiny channels close up). This means cool to lukewarm water to rinse the towel with as you're working, and the "cool" or "cold" setting on the washing machine.
- **NEVER** expose the microfiber towel to heat. Use the coolest ("delicate") setting on the dryer, don't iron it (why would anyone?) and don't use it on hot objects. With high temperatures the synthetic fibers will melt.
- **NEVER** use a fabric softener with a microfiber towel. Not in the washer and not in the dryer. The chemicals in the softeners will coat the microfibers, keeping them from working like they should.
- **NEVER** wash a microfiber towel with regular terry cloth towels, socks or other items that shed a lot of lint. The microfiber towel will pick up the lint from cotton towels and get clogged up. Instead, wash the microfiber towels in a load with other fabrics that also need cool water. What I have learned is that the towels actually wash up the best if you do a load of just the microfiber towels, using about ¼ as much laundry detergent as for a regular load. The towels need lots of water, though so only put about half as many in the wash as you would with regular fabrics. I tested a load just going through the rinse cycle with four towels, and they were just about as clean as the ones that had gone through the wash cycle too.
- **AVOID** powdered laundry products since some of them don't dissolve all of the way and detergent grains can get picked up by the microfibers. The same is true if you want to use a disinfectant with the towel—stick to the liquids. You can add bleach to the wash load, but only use about half as much as you would for bleaching whites. (The exact amount will depend on how large your washing machine is.)

By learning to use microfiber towels, you can avoid using many household cleaning chemicals and contribute to cleaner air and water as well as having a super-green clean home. Microfiber towels leave surfaces cleaner than conventional methods so things stay cleaner longer, too. To learn more about how these towels work, see *The Super-Green Clean: Using Microfiber Towels to Clean Nearly Anything with Plain Water,* by Applaloosa Moose. The book is available online at Amazon.com and Barnes & Noble.

Printed in the United States
30588LVS00006B/655-753

9 781931 426404